GOSPEL OF LUKE SCRIPTURE STUDY

THE PRODIGAL SON

AND

Augustine of Hippo

An 6-part Scripture study of Luke 15:1-32

Creator and Writer: Kristina Romero
Book Design and Layout: John Falke, Julie Falke, Judan Jaymelensonn
Research and Development: Kristina Romero

ISBN-13: 979-8-9852372-2-1

Cover image is of the ruins of ancient Hippo and the St Augustine Basilica in Annaba,
Algeria. A special thank you and credit to Kristen Hellstrom, Director ASA Cultural Tours

Contents

GET THE FREE MOBILE APP

Scan the QR code to install **The Hagios Study** mobile app full of audio and video meditations used in the study.

How to use this study

Before you begin, take some time to review the distinctive features of a Hagios Study crafted to enhance your journey. These include utilizing the free mobile app for meditation, engaging with each part's four Lectio Divina sections, designated parts for journaling, ample sidebar space for note-taking, and questions for deeper analysis or discussion.

APP PROMPT

These prompts encourage you to visit our free mobile app to enhance your journey through audio-visuals. View the previous page for directions on downloading the app or visit https://hagios.study/app

READ, REFLECT, RESPOND, REST

Each section follows the ancient Lectio Divina method for scripture study. You can do all four sections in one day or break them up over a week. View the following page on how each of the four sections is structured.

JOURNAL

This study encourages journaling and note-taking. These "Reflect Notes" sections are for you to record your thoughts and observations.

SIDEBAR

The sidebars are specifically designed for note-taking. Use this space to highlight verses, journal thoughts, or add comments.

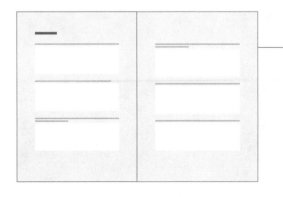

QUESTIONS

Each part includes a question section meant to encourage contemplation, analysis, and reflection. These questions are also ideal to discuss in a small group setting.

Section Breakdowns

Each of the four sections follow the ancient monastic form of studying scripture called Lectio Divina, Latin for "divine reading." The prayerful practice was first established in the 6th century by Benedict of Nursia and then fleshed out into a four-step process by the Carthusian monk Guigo II in the 12th century. The purpose of the format for Lectio Divina is to enter into a conversation with God.

Since this study is a scripture study, we will use the Lectio Divina scholastic format of Reading, Reflecting, Responding, and Resting. In each section, we seek to be guided by the Holy Spirit. There's plenty of flexibility in how you execute your week. If you'd like to do one section a day or all four in one day, that's up to how the Spirit is leading you.

The goal of Lectio Divina is to make scripture come alive and provide a way for you to connect with God's Word on a level that is both personal and convicting.

THE LADDER OF FOUR RUNGS

Reading seeks,
meditation finds,
prayer asks,
contemplation feels.

Reading puts as it were whole food into your mouth;
meditation chews it and breaks it down;
prayer finds its savour;
contemplation is the sweetness that so delights and strengthens.

Reading is like the bark, the shell;
meditation like the pith, the nut;
prayer is in the desiring asking;
and contemplation is in the delight of the great sweetness

- Guigo II, Carthusian monk in the 12th Century (1140-1193)

READ

"Reading seeks..." The READ section explores the featured verse by viewing it alongside supporting verses that include shared keywords. By comparing the same words across the Greek versions of the Old and New Testament we can better understand the English translation and how these parallel verses give insight into the main reading. In READ, we encourage you to take in the information intellectually before you move into REFLECT. As Guigo II noted, "Reading puts, as it were, whole food into your mouth."

 # REFLECT

"Meditation finds..." The REFLECT section offers up a skillfully crafted meditation video on the Hagios Study mobile app along with short reflections from ancient Church Fathers to aid you in discovering how to apply the scripture verse to your life. This section encourages you to seek out a moment of meditation before you seek to RESPOND. In REFLECT, ask the Holy Spirit to reveal to you what He wants to say to you, then journal your notes down in the space provided. Let the presented reflections and experiential meditation in our mobile app give you the means to "chew it and break it down."

 # RESPOND

"Prayer asks…" The RESPOND section unfolds a story of response in the life of a Christian brethren with questions desired to aid you in prayerfully determining an application to your life. RESPOND becomes a means for you to discover deeper reflection on yourself through the witness of another in our communion of saints. Through a study of another's life as a response to scripture, you will "find its savour" to determine how the Holy Spirit is leading you.

♡ REST

"Contemplation feels…" The final section REST brings together all the previous three sections for a moment of final considerations. In REST are two ways for you to settle into "the sweetness that so delights and strengthens." Begin by listening to a contemporary praise song on the mobile app while meditating on the verses from the READ section. Then finish with an inspired prayer from our communion of saints. REST will encourage you to digest all the Holy Spirit has revealed to you throughout the week as you move along your journey through the study.

"

Now all the tax collectors and sinners were coming near to listen to him. And the Pharisees and the scribes were grumbling and saying, "This fellow welcomes sinners and eats with them."

Image: The ruins of the Ophel walls and the place where the first and second Temple complex was located, Jerusalem, Israel

LUKE 15:1 -2 (NRSV)

Introduction

On a quiet day in Milan, Italy, at the end of the 4th century, the wayward Augustine paced through his garden. He was conflicted, agonizing at his reluctance to surrender a lifestyle of worldly ambition and lust that had consumed him. As he cried out to God in tears, he heard a child's voice in a neighboring garden sing, "Pick it up and read, pick it up and read."[1] Taking that prompt literally, Augustine picked up a nearby Biblical text on a table from St. Paul and arrived immediately in Romans 13:

"Let us then lay aside the works of darkness and put on the armor of light; let us live honorably as in the day, not in reveling and drunkenness, not in debauchery and licentiousness, not in quarreling and jealousy. Instead, put on the Lord Jesus Christ, and make no provision for the flesh, to gratify its desires" (Romans 13:12-14)

As Augustine writes in his autobiography, *The Confessions*,

"No sooner had I reached the end of the verse than the light of certainty flooded my heart, and all dark shades of doubt fled away."[2]

With no need to read a single word more, he resolved to come home to the Father. Augustine would go on to become one of the most celebrated intellectual minds of all Christianity and a Church Father who conceptualized significant doctrine and theology. He would embody the quintessential "prodigal son," lured away by a corrupted world with an incredible conversion aided by his mother's urgent prayers.

The Parable of the Prodigal Son was Jesus' response to inquisitive Pharisees (a Jewish religious sect) who questioned why Jesus would eat with sinners and tax collectors. His response in the parable is a simple lesson: He was returning the lost to the God the Father. This parable is full of substance despite its simplicity. It has become one of the most popular and recited parables in the New Testament.

Likewise, Augustine of Hippo has become one of the most loved Christians throughout Christian history and one of the few from the early Church we know so much about, thanks to his writings. *The Confessions*, his premier auto-biographical work, can best be described as "one long prayer–a poetic, passionate, intimate prayer."[3]

In 397 AD, at age forty-three, Augustine wrote *The Confessions*. He had only been baptized into the Church ten years prior. More remarkably, he had only been a priest for six years and a bishop for two. Yet his wisdom and skill in communicating his conversion story rival that of theologians with a lifetime of experience.

Although Augustine was an intellectual, *The Confessions* is full of heartfelt emotion. It is a unique outpouring of his sorrows, passions, and regrets. *The Confessions* wasn't a personal diary. He wrote it to be public and have it read aloud to groups of listeners. Despite it being an autobiography, it doesn't read like a vanity piece but rather a candid and intimate revelation of his memories.

Augustine's way to God begins as a pursuit of self-knowledge and ends with a humble receipt of mercy. This parallels the prodigal son in Luke 15, who "comes to himself" before returning to the loving father's embrace.

By viewing the Parable of the Lost Sheep, Lost Coin, and Lost Son (or Prodigal Son) through the eyes of Augustine's life as chronicled in his *Confessions*, this 6-part study will help you uncover a deeper understanding of yourself and your own journey home.

SECTIONS OF THE STUDY

Each part begins with "Read," looking at a keyword from a select passage in Luke 15. After which is "Reflect," a time to meditate on these verses with music from the mobile app and commentary from an early Church Father.

St. Ambrose's commentary on Luke 15 occupies most of the "Reflect" sections, which is by design. Through Ambrose's preaching, Augustine's heart and mind aligned in finally understanding the scripture. Therefore, lean on Ambrose's insights as you journal your own thoughts.

Next, is "Respond," how Augustine's life is a response to these verses. Using his own words from *The Confessions*, "Respond" draws a parallel between the prodigal son and Augustine, giving flesh to the man from the parable. Its as if it was Augustine himself Christ was describing.

Then, you have the final section "Rest," a time to pull all your insights together in prayer. In this study the "Rest" prayers are pulled straight from Augustine's *Confessions*. These poetic excerpts pair well with the Rest meditations songs located on the companion mobile app.

In this study you will pilgrimage with Augustine from the serene town of Thagaste in Northern Africa, where he was born, to the crowded gladiator arenas of Carthage where he taught rhetoric. You will then journey to Milan's cathedral walls where Ambrose's inspired words caught his ear and ignited his heart. Finally, you'll arrive back in Northern Africa, in the ancient city of Hippo where Augustine sings God's praises at the end of his life.

Gary Wills, a noted author on St. Augustine's life, once wrote, "Augustine did not delve into his soul to find sin. He went there to find God - and he did."[4]

The same can apply to this study. It aims not to dwell on the darkness of sin or ways we have turned from God, but to guide our memory in recognizing acts of His mercy. Through these pages, may you discover the loving Father running toward you on the road of redemption and be moved by His celebration of your return.

Jesus' Ministry in Luke

Jesus began His ministry in the region of Galilee in Northern Israel. During His ministry in Jerusalem he preaches, performs miracles and tells many parables. It is there in Jerusalem where He is was crucified, resurrects and ascends to Heaven.

BORN IN BETHLEHEM
est 4-6 BC Luke 2

BOY JESUS IS FOUND IN THE TEMPLE
8 AD Luke 2

BAPTIZED BY JOHN
26 AD Luke 3

JESUS CALLS HIS FIRST DISCIPLES
27 AD Luke 4-5

MINISTRY AND HEALINGS
27-30 AD Luke 5-18

THE PARABLE OF THE LOST SHEEP, LOST COIN & LOST SON
30 AD Luke 15

PALM SUNDAY, ENTRY INTO JERUSALEM
30 AD Luke 19

FINAL PASSOVER AND BETRAYAL
30 AD Luke 22

JESUS' CRUCIFIXION
30 AD Luke 23

JESUS' RESURRECTION
30 AD Luke 24

Augustine's Conversion

Augustine was born in Northern Africa only a few decades after the Roman empire ended its persecution of Christians. He went onto become one of the greatest intellectual minds of Christianity, with his premier work *The Confessions* detailing his conversion story.

BORN IN THAGASTE, AFRICA
354 AD

STUDIES RHETORIC IN CARTHAGE
371 AD

FATHERS DIES, ADEODATUS IS BORN
372-373 AD

SAILS TO ROME FOR CAREER
383 AD

TEACHES IN MILAN, MEETS AMBROSE
384 AD

CONVERTS TO CHRISTIANITY
386 AD

AUGUSTINE IS BAPTIZED AND HIS MOTHER MONICA DIES
387 AD

BECOMES BISHOP OF HIPPO
396 AD

WRITES *THE CONFESSIONS*
400 AD

DIES IN HIPPO
Aug 28, 430 AD

AUGUSTINE IS CANONIZED BY POPE BONIFACE VIII
1303 AD

Scripture

LUKE 15:1-32

[1] Now all the tax-collectors and sinners were coming near to listen to him. [2] And the Pharisees and the scribes were grumbling and saying, 'This fellow welcomes sinners and eats with them.'

[3] So he told them this parable: [4] 'Which one of you, having a hundred sheep and losing one of them, does not leave the ninety-nine in the wilderness and go after the one that is lost until he finds it? [5] When he has found it, he lays it on his shoulders and rejoices. [6] And when he comes home, he calls together his friends and neighbours, saying to them, "Rejoice with me, for I have found my sheep that was lost." [7] Just so, I tell you, there will be more joy in heaven over one sinner who repents than over ninety-nine righteous people who need no repentance.

[8] 'Or what woman having ten silver coins, if she loses one of them, does not light a lamp, sweep the house, and search carefully until she finds it? [9] When she has found it, she calls together her friends and neighbours, saying, "Rejoice with me, for I have found the coin that I had lost." [10] Just so, I tell you, there is joy in the presence of the angels of God over one sinner who repents.'

[11] Then Jesus said, 'There was a man who had two sons. [12] The younger of them said to his father, "Father, give me the share of the property that will belong to me." So he divided his property between them. [13] A few days later the younger son gathered all he had and travelled to a distant country, and there he squandered his property in dissolute living. [14] When he had spent everything, a severe famine took place throughout that country, and he began to be in need. [15] So he went and hired himself out to one of the citizens of that country, who sent him to his fields to feed the pigs. [16] He would gladly have filled himself with the pods that the pigs were eating; and no one gave him anything. [17] But when he came to himself he said, "How many of my father's hired hands have bread enough and to spare, but here I am dying of hunger! [18] I will get up and go to my father, and I will say to him, 'Father, I have sinned against heaven and before you; [19] I am no longer worthy to be called your son; treat me like one of your hired hands.'"

Image: Shepherd caring for sheep in Turkey

²⁰ So he set off and went to his father. But while he was still far off, his father saw him and was filled with compassion; he ran and put his arms around him and kissed him. ²¹ Then the son said to him, "Father, I have sinned against heaven and before you; I am no longer worthy to be called your son."

²² But the father said to his slaves, "Quickly, bring out a robe—the best one—and put it on him; put a ring on his finger and sandals on his feet. ²³ And get the fatted calf and kill it, and let us eat and celebrate; ²⁴ for this son of mine was dead and is alive again; he was lost and is found!" And they began to celebrate.

²⁵ 'Now his elder son was in the field; and when he came and approached the house, he heard music and dancing. ²⁶ He called one of the slaves and asked what was going on. ²⁷ He replied, "Your brother has come, and your father has killed the fatted calf, because he has got him back safe and sound."

²⁸ Then he became angry and refused to go in. His father came out and began to plead with him. ²⁹ But he answered his father, "Listen! For all these years I have been working like a slave for you, and I have never disobeyed your command; yet you have never given me even a young goat so that I might celebrate with my friends. ³⁰ But when this son of yours came back, who has devoured your property with prostitutes, you killed the fatted calf for him!"

³¹ Then the father said to him, "Son, you are always with me, and all that is mine is yours. ³² But we had to celebrate and rejoice, because this brother of yours was dead and has come to life; he was lost and has been found."'

(NRSV)

The Hagios Study quotes Scripture from The New Revised Standard Version of the Bible (NRSV). This translation was published in 1989 and has received the widest acclaim and broadest support from academics and church leaders of any modern English translation.

Image: Ruins of the Domitian gates in the ancient city of Hierapolis, Turkey

Image: Panoramic view of ancient Jerusalem and surrounding area

PART 1

—

Lost Spaces

"

Which one of you, having a hundred sheep and losing one of them, does not leave the ninety-nine in the wilderness and go after the one that is lost until he finds it?

LUKE 15:4 (NRSV)

Read

DEEP DIVE INTO SCRIPTURE

Read Luke15:1-8 "… which one of you, having a hundred sheep and losing one of them, does not leave the ninety-nine in the wilderness and go after the one that is lost until he finds it?…" In order to study verses 1-8, look up supporting verses below that also include the word "lost." Since the New Testament was written in Greek, parallel verses that use the same Greek word for lost (*apollumi*) are listed for you. Using your own Bible translation, read and write out these verses.

Word / Phrase	Verse	Write Out His Word
to lose, to perish, to destroy (English) apollumi (Greek)	Psalm 119:176	
	Jeremiah 50:6	
	Ezekiel 34:16	
	Luke 9:25	
	John 10:10	

A LOST PEOPLE

When Jesus began sharing the parable of the lost sheep, the lost coin, and the lost son in Luke chapter 15, He tapped into a concept familiar to the Pharisees—the idea of being lost and sought after by God. Throughout the Greek Old Testament, there are numerous references to being lost, using the Greek word *apollymi*.

The word *apollymi* (pronounced ap-ol'-loo-mee) carries a deeper meaning than mere temporary misplacement or loss. It encompasses the notion of being lost forever or destroyed. It implies a state of utter devastation. In English, *apollymi* is defined as "to destroy fully (reflexively, to perish, or lose), literally or figuratively."[1]

apollymi - to lose, to destroy, to perish

By intentionally utilizing this specific word, Jesus captured the attention of His audience, setting the stage for the surprising revelation that even the seemingly irretrievable can be found. As he explains the ease of retrieving the lost sheep and then the lost coin, He carefully sets up the extraordinary redemption that would be displayed in the prodigal son's story.

Looking back through the Greek Old Testament, searching for the word *apollymi* uncovers supporting verses that shed light on how listeners in Jesus' day would have reacted to the parable.

In Psalm 119, King David, even though being known as a man after God's own heart, expressed his personal experience of feeling lost. He compared himself to a lost sheep, acknowledging his need for God's guidance and seeking His servant's restoration:

"I have gone astray like a lost (*apollymi*) sheep; seek out your servant, for I do not forget your commandments."
Psalm 119:176

Through this heartfelt expression, David recognizes the significance of God's role as the shepherd who seeks and restores the lost.

The prophet Jeremiah, who lived during a time of great turmoil and destruction, conveyed the imagery of Israel as lost sheep. He delivered God's message, highlighting the consequences of the nation's spiritual wandering and the responsibility of their shepherds in leading them astray:

"My people have been lost (*apollymi*) sheep; their shepherds have led them astray, turning them away on the mountains; from mountain to hill they have gone, they have forgotten their fold." Jeremiah 50:6

Jeremiah's words reveal the longing of God to gather His people back into His loving care. He will guide them back to their rightful place.

Likewise, the prophet Ezekiel, who ministered during the Babylonian exile, emphasized God's role as the seeking and restoring shepherd. In a time of immense hardship and despair, Ezekiel conveyed God's promise to search for the lost, tend to the wounded, and strengthen the weak. He contrasted the restoration of the lost with the judgment for those whose hearts are hardened:

"I will seek the lost (*apollymi*), and I will bring back the strayed, and I will bind up the injured, and I will strengthen the weak, but the fat and the strong I will destroy. I will feed them with justice."

| Ezekiel 34:16

Ezekiel's message offered hope and comfort to the exiled Israelites, assuring them of God's faithfulness and His desire to restore them despite their current state.

While the Old Testament speaks often of returning the lost for physical safety and prosperity, in the New Testament Jesus points to the spiritual. He challenges the disciples' perspective on worldly gain as He poses the question,

| "What does it profit them if they gain the whole world but lose (*apollymi)* or forfeit themselves?" Luke 9:25

Throughout the Gospels, Jesus consistently highlights that those who are lost often find themselves in such a state due to being led astray.

| "The thief comes only to steal and kill and destroy (*apollymi*). I have come that they may have life, and have it to the full." John 10:10

Implying more than mere loss but complete destruction, Jesus points to the redemption that can only be attained through His sacrificial act—a restoration of what was lost. For this spiritual reason, he asserts His mission proclaiming,

| "For the Son of Man came to seek out and to save the lost (*apollymi)*." Luke 19:10

This is repeated in additional books of the New Testament, like the apostle James, who addressed the theme of judgment and restoration in his letter. James wrote to Jewish believers scattered throughout various regions, urging them to live out their faith authentically and to avoid judging others.

| "There is one lawgiver and judge who is able to save and to destroy (*apollymi)*. So who, then, are you to judge your neighbor?" James 4:12

By invoking the concept of judgment and restoration, James conveyed the need for humility and the avoidance of self-righteousness, a potential reference back to the motivation of the Pharisees who's inquiry spurred the parable.

Through the combined perspectives of the Old Testament writings of King David, the prophets Jeremiah and Ezekiel, coupled with the words of Christ in the New Testament, a comprehensive understanding of "the lost" (*apollymi)* emerges.

While we may not know the specific circumstances that led a sheep to wander onto a distant hill, caused a coin to slip between the cracks of a floorboard, or enticed the prodigal son to stray, we can find assurance in Christ's words that restoration is possible. Despite the state of destruction, Christ, the Good Shepherd, is present among the lost, actively seeking to bring them back home.

Reflect

on the app . . .

VISIT THIS SECTION'S MEDITATION VIDEO IN THE APP FOR A MOMENT OF GUIDED REFLECTION

REFLECTION FROM AN EARLY CHURCH FATHER

" The world is a slippery place. It is hard for human nature to keep its footsteps firm. So the Good Physician has His remedies for those who go astray and once again He shows these to you. This merciful Judge holds out to you the hope of pardon. Saint Luke has a very deliberate purpose in proposing to you these three parables that follow one after the other: the sheep that went astray and was found; the drachma [coin] that was lost and recovered; the son that was dead and was restored to life. By this triple remedy He undertakes to cure you of your wounds…

Who are they, this father, this shepherd, this woman? I would say that the father is God, the shepherd is Christ, and the woman is the Church. Christ carries you on His own shoulder, having taken on Himself your sins; the Church goes looking for you; the Father welcomes you. As a shepherd He carries you, as a mother He searches for you, as a father He clothes you. In the first place comes mercy, then follows assistance, and thirdly there is reconciliation. Every detail fits perfectly into place: the Redeemer comes to our help, the Church assists us, the Father is reconciled with us…

We ought to be happy, very happy, that the sheep which was lost in Adam is recovered in Christ. Christ's shoulders are the arms of the Cross. It is there that I lay down my burden of sins. On the noble neck of Christ's gibbet I rest my head…

We are sheep. Let us ask Him to be so kind as to lead us to the waters that revive the spirit. I repeat it, we are sheep; let us beg Him to give us pastures green. We are drachmas, let us keep our value. We are children, let us run to the Father.

- St. Ambrose, *Exposition on the Gospel of St. Luke*, Book VII (377 AD)

As you ponder these verses, journal your thoughts in the space provided. Reflect on the scripture passage (and subsequent supporting passages) from "Read." Is there a word that stands out? What do these verses mean to you? What is the Holy Spirit showing you in these scripture passages?

LOST SPACES

Image: View of Thagaste where Augustine wa
born. Souk Ahras, Algeria. Credit: Amina
STITI, CC BY-SA 4.0, via Wikimedia Comm

Respond

In this section, we will learn from Augustine of Hippo and his response to God's word. May it serve as example as you seek out how the Holy Spirit is prompting you to Respond.

WANDERING IN LOST SPACES

Augustine's famous autobiography is, in fact, not an autobiography at all. Instead, it is a prayer directed at God to inspire others to rejoice and praise the Father. The work's first words proclaim:

> "Great are you, O Lord, and exceedingly worthy of praise; your power is immense, and your wisdom beyond reckoning …You stir us so that praising you may bring us joy, because you have made us and drawn us to yourself, and our heart is unquiet until it rests in you."[2]

With this open letter of praise, Augustine places God as the main character as he attempts to return to his memory, confessing his past and drawing a powerful parallel between him and the rebellious son in Christ's parable. Written only ten years after becoming a Christian, Augustine shares candidly in hopes that his tales of waywardness can be a story that convinces others of God's mercy.

Augustine grew up in Thagaste, Northern Africa, present-day Algeria. In Augustine's time, Northern Africa was part of the Roman world in both rule and culture. Christianity had only been a legal religion for forty years. Though widely accepted, it suffered from heated disagreements.

There were two prominent Christian theological viewpoints during Augustine's lifetime. The Arian view demoted Christ to be separate in His relation and authority to God. The Catholic Trinitarian doctrine upheld Christ's divinity as the same in being with God. This critical debate influences much of Augustine's writings on Christ's nature. This passion for defending true doctrine underlines much of *The Confessions* as he observes the Catholic Church's struggle to find its footing in a sea of controversy (with Arianism, Donatism, Pelagianism, and others).

Augustine was born into a Catholic Christian home. His mother, Monica, was a faithful believer, while his father, although pagan initially, became a Christian shortly before his death when Augustine was a teenager. Despite this, Augustine recounts a childhood where virtue took a back seat in emphasis to his education and worldly success.

> "The program for right living presented to me as a boy was that I must obey my mentors so that I might get on in the world and excel in the skills of the tongue."[3]

Early in his youth, he learned skillful language, leveraging words, thoughts, and arguments to get his way. Augustine writes how these words inspired his intellect, but did not help him with virtue as this talent only encouraged his pride.

He was punished for disobedience, for

playing when he was supposed to learn. Augustine marvels at the hypocrisy of his teachers, who nonetheless did the same themselves. As much as education was of significant value to the Roman world, he describes a culture obsessed with entertainment through games, plays, and stories.

"The people who provide these entertainments enjoy such celebrity and public esteem that nearly all of them hope their children will follow their example; and yet they are quite prepared to see those children beaten for watching similar shows to the detriment of their study, study which, as their parents hope, will bring them to a position in which they, in turn, will provide the shows!"[4]

In many ways, the world in which he was born did not set up a priority to love the heavenly Father. Instead, ambitions tugged on the weakness of his soul to satisfy the pull with all the world could offer.

In his youth, his sin of pride was exhibited in typical disobedience, getting in trouble in class, and talking back. He complained about learning Greek and frequently defied his teachers and parents. Augustine illustrates it simply by stating that he was "a great sinner for such a tiny boy."[5]

Augustine began to wander further from truth through his obsession with stories and how they made him feel. These plays and written works would drive him to tears, stoking a desire to love and be loved like the characters in the fantasies. It was a struggle, he writes, to choose virtue over these pursuits as these stories and cleverly crafted speeches were celebrated. Augustine recalls:

"To pander to this world is to fornicate against you [Lord], but so loudly do they shout, 'Well done!'"[6]

Augustine, in his youth, longed for and desired praise. Praise, he says, better directed toward God. He writes,

"I believed that living a good life consisted in winning the favor of those who commended me. I was earning the disapproval even of those same people by the countless lies with which I deceived the slave who took me to school, my teachers, my parents, and all because of my love for play and the absurd anxiety with which I craved to gawk at worthless shows and imitate what I watched."[7]

Despite this repeated deception, Augustine didn't find much pushback, especially from his teachers. His education was full of stories encouraging Augustine's behavior, tales used to teach the basics of grammar and speech. The teachers were just as deceived by this culture and rewarded those who consumed such obscene stories. He adds,

"I learned these things eagerly and took pleasure in them; and so I was accounted a boy of high promise."[8]

Augustine's gift of words became a powerful tool to manipulate. He lied and, when confronted, had a hot temper.

Then, at sixteen, Augustine recalls a significant acceleration point in his wandering away from God. Augustine discovers lust, or as he better describes it, "in love with loving."[9] Where Augustine may have been reduced from such errors of affairs with women by his family arranging a marriage, they held off for the sake of his career. Despite not being particularly wealthy as the town councilor of Thagaste, his father had saved a significant amount of money to send him to the best school in Carthage. A marriage, it seems, would complicate those plans.

While his father laughs off Augustine's interest with the opposite sex, his mother, Monica, slowly awakens to a shift in the state of her son's soul. She intervenes and cautions him, but Augustine blows her off.

> "By using her [Lord], you were not silent to me at all: and when I scorned her, I was scorning you."[10]

Augustine even boasts about obscene behavior with his friends, although he's innocent of most conduct he brags about.

Then, at seventeen, Augustine's ways catch up to him and he fathers a son, Adeodatus. Despite this, Monica refuses to arrange a marriage.

> "[She feared] that if I were encumbered with a wife, my hope could be dashed–not hope in you [God] for the world to come, to which she held herself, but my hope of academic success."[11]

To highlight the grotesque nature of his sin, Augustine describes a relatively innocent act of stealing pears from a neighbor's tree. For Augustine, it was a grievous sin because he was stealing for the sake of destroying. He had no use for the pears, plucking them from the tree with his friends and throwing them away.

> "... those pears we stole did have a certain beauty because they were your creation-yours, O God, who are the highest good and the true good for me. Those pears were beautiful, but they were not what my miserable soul loved. I had plenty of better ones, and I

plucked them only for the sake of stealing, for once picked, I threw them away. I feasted on the sin, nothing else, and that I relished and enjoyed."[12]

In all these memories, Augustine highlights the beauty of God exhibited in His creation through enlightened education, powerful stories of love and loss, the female form, and even in pears. Though it is God's work which is good, sin perverts it all.

> "All those who wander far away and set themselves up against you are imitating you, but in a perverse way."[13]

As Augustine grew and went off to school in Carthage, he plunged "into the treacherous abyss, into depths of unbelief."[14] At nineteen, he realizes the emptiness of his adolescent pursuits and attempts to read the Holy Scriptures. Yet at this point in his life, it does not pierce his heart. He is disappointed by it's literary style and incapable of seeing its application to his life.

> "My swollen pride recoiled from its style, and my intelligence failed to penetrate to its inner meaning."[15]

With a craving for meaning the world offers, he turns to Cicero and philosophy. This interest kindles an insatiable appetite for the truth in the wrong direction.

QUESTIONS

1. Why do you think Augustine writes *The Confessions*? What does he hope to convey?

2. Where were some of Augustine's lost spaces?

3. What factors does Augustine say encouraged him toward sin?

4. In what ways is ancient Rome at the time of Augustine similar to today?

5. What are some times in your life you felt lost?

6. What ways can you help others who are struggling to find God from lost places?

"*I have gone astray like a lost sheep; seek out your servant, for I do not forget your commandments.*"

PSALM 119:176 ((NRSV)

Image: Below the Church of the Holy Sepulch
the site of the Crucifixion, Jerusalem, Israel

Rest

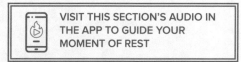

VISIT THIS SECTION'S AUDIO IN THE APP TO GUIDE YOUR MOMENT OF REST

As you finish this part of the study, visit the mobile app for this section's Rest meditation song. Additionally, below is an excerpt from Augustine's *Confessions* to give perspective on longing for God from lost spaces.

TO SEEK AND FIND

The words of your holy scripture have knocked at the door of my heart, O Lord, and in this poverty-stricken life of mine my heart is busy about many things concerning them.

The poverty of human understanding is apt to lead to excessive wordiness, for to seek requires more talking than to find, to ask takes longer than to obtain, and the hand that knocks puts in more effort than the hand that receives.

But we cling to your promise: who shall rob it of its force? If God is for us, who is against us?

Ask, and you will obtain; seek, and you will find; knock, and the door will be opened to you. For everyone who asks, obtains, and the seeker will find, and to the one who knocks the door will be opened: these are your promises; and who need fear to be deceived by the promises of Truth himself?

- Augustine of Hippo, *The Confessions*, Book XII, Section 1

PART 2 - SEVERE FAMINE

Image: View overlooking the red sand desert th
Israelites wandered in Wadi Rum, Jordan

PART 2

Severe Famine

> When he had spent everything, a severe famine took place throughout that country, and he began to be in need.

LUKE 15:14 (NRSV)

Image: Ancient stone mill used to grind grain

Read

DEEP DIVE INTO SCRIPTURE

Read Luke 15:11-14 "Then Jesus said, 'There was a man who had two sons…'" As you examine verses 11-14, write out the supporting verses from both the Old and New Testament that used the same Greek word for the state of "being in need" (*hystereō*). Use your preferred translation and make note of any different English words used.

Word / Phrase	Verse	Write Out His Word
to lack, to suffer need, impoverished, destitute (English) hystereō (Greek)	Nehemiah 9:21	
	Ecclesiastes 6:1-2	
	Matthew 19: 20-22	
	Romans 3:23	
	Philippians 4:12	

THOSE IN NEED

The son's realization in verses 11-14 distinctly differs from the lack of awareness demonstrated by the sheep and the coin. The sheep and the coin play no active role in their return. They are rescued despite their actions or inaction.

However, in the son's story, he experiences a personal awakening arising from a deep need. The word used for need in Greek is *hystereō*.

hystereō (Greek) - to lack, fall short, to suffer need, impoverished, destitute

The term *hystereō* (pronounced hoos-ter-eh'-o) conveys a sense of being utterly impoverished, lacking, and in a state of suffering need.[1] The famine that befalls the son serves as a circumstance that highlights an actual spiritual condition.

Hystereō is often used in scripture as a synonym for sin and in other verses to describe failure.

The imagery of famine in the parable evokes the memory of the Israelites wandering in the desert, as their need is what turns them back to God. Despite their weariness and complaints, God continued to provide for them. The prophet Nehemiah reflects on this provision writing:

> "Forty years you sustained them in the wilderness so that they lacked (*hystereō*) nothing; their clothes did not wear out and their feet did not swell." Nehemiah 9:21

This narrative underscores the theme that the Lord is the source of everything we truly need. When we stray too far, seeking only the riches and possessions that the world offers, we become strangers to our eternal home. As Ecclesiastes wisely states:

> "There is an evil that I have seen under the sun, and it lies heavy upon humankind: those to whom God gives wealth, possessions, and honor, so that they lack (*hystereō*) nothing of all that they desire, yet God does not enable them to enjoy these things, but a stranger enjoys them. This is vanity; it is a grievous ill." Ecclesiastes 6:1-2

This passage foreshadows the encounter between Jesus and the rich man who approached Him seeking eternal life. The young man declared his adherence to the commandments but still felt a lack within himself. Jesus then challenges him to sell his possessions, give to the poor, and follow Him.

> "The young man said to him, 'I have kept all these; what do I still lack (*hystereō*)?' Jesus said to him, 'If you wish to be perfect, go, sell your possessions, and give the money to the poor, and you will have treasure in heaven; then come, follow me.' When the young man heard this word, he went away grieving, for he had many possessions." Matthew 19: 20-22

This passage emphasizes the call to recognize our spiritual poverty and the emptiness that material wealth alone cannot fill. In the case of the prodigal son, only when he reaches a state of famine can his soul be illuminated to its shortcomings.

The same Greek word *hystereō* used in these passages, is also found in the letter to the Romans as a reason we need Christ:

> "But now, apart from law, the righteousness of God has been

disclosed, and is attested by the law and the prophets, the righteousness of God through faith in Jesus Christ for all who believe. For there is no distinction, since all have sinned and fall short (*hystereō*) of the glory of God;" Romans 3:21-23

Whether we realize it or not, we are unable to come home on our own. We need the Good Shepherd. That is precisely why God sent His Son to die for us.

The concept of being in need isn't just spiritual lack, but also physical when considering our earthly circumstances and human realities. The words of the apostle Paul further exemplify this connection in his letter to the Philippians. He expresses firsthand experience of both scarcity and abundance, learning the secret of contentment.

"I know what it is to have little, and I know what it is to have plenty. In any and all circumstances I have learned the secret of being well-fed and of going hungry, of having plenty and of being in need (*hystereō*)." Philippians 4:12

Paul's joyful declaration reveals the transformative power of recognizing all you lack and relying on God's provisions in every aspect of life.

Similarly, in the first letter to the Corinthians, Paul assures the believers that they have Christ with them on their journey, having everything they need.

"for in every way you have been enriched in him, in speech and knowledge of every kind— just as the testimony of Christ has been strengthened among you— so that you are not lacking (*hystereō)* in any spiritual gift as you wait for the revealing of our Lord Jesus Christ. He will also strengthen you to the end, so that you may be blameless on the day of our Lord Jesus Christ." 1 Corinthians 1:5-8

Paul's message emphasizes that we have what's necessary to navigate life's challenges on the way to our eternal home. Through the strength and guidance of the Holy Spirit, we can find support and contentment on our pilgrimage.

We live in a world full of distractions to artificially satisfy our needs and desires. The famine of earthly circumstances can often encroach upon our joy, causing us to forget the promises of Christ.

Yet, let us remember we have access to substantial provisions, ever-present through the Holy Spirit, and ultimately found in the loving embrace of our heavenly Father, who awaits our return.

Reflect

on the app...

VISIT THIS SECTION'S MEDITATION VIDEO IN THE APP FOR A MOMENT OF GUIDED REFLECTION

REFLECTION FROM AN EARLY CHURCH FATHER

" There came a mighty famine in that country" (Lk 15:14). This was not a scarcity of food, but a collapse of good works and of virtues. Can any famine be sadder than that? Truly, anyone who deserts the word of God, is gnawed by hunger. For "we do not live on bread alone, but on every word that comes from the mouth of God" (Lk 4:4). If you cut yourself off from the fountain, you are thirsty; if you cut yourself off from the treasure, you are poor; if you cut yourself off from wisdom you are stupid; and if you cut yourself off from virtue you are destroyed. This youth had left behind him the treasures of wisdom and of the knowledge of God, and it is scarcely surprising that he began to suffer want. He had made himself a stranger to the depths of the heavenly riches. He suffered want and was hungry because insatiable thirst for pleasure never has enough. Those who are unwilling to fill themselves with the food that is eternal, will always suffer hunger.

Debauched people care only to fill their belly, for "their belly is their god" (Ph 3:19). Husks are most suitable for people of this sort, for husks are soft on the outside,

containing nothing on the inside. They fill the body, but do not nourish it. They weigh down the system without being of any use to it.

Some people see the swine as representing troops of demons; they see the husks as the puny virtue of speakers intoxicated by their vain, empty and useless verbosity. By the foolish seduction of clever talk, by their fine flow of fancy eloquence, by the noise they make, these "philosophers" tickle the ear rather than produce anything of real use and lasting worth.

- St. Ambrose, *Exposition on the Gospel of St. Luke*, Book VII (377 AD)

As you ponder these verses, journal your thoughts in the space provided. Reflect on the scripture passage (and subsequent supporting passages) from "Read." Is there a word that stands out? What do these verses mean to you? What is the Holy Spirit showing you in these scripture passages?

SEVERE FAMINE

Image: Park of the Via Latina Tombs, an ancie
piece of the Appian way, Rome, Italy

Respond

In this section, we will continue our look at Augustine of Hippo and his response to God's word. May it serve as example as you seek out how the Holy Spirit is prompting you to Respond.

RUNNING TOWARD DISCONTENT

As Augustine remained in his lost spaces, it caused an increase in him feelings of restlessness and discontent. In his early adulthood, all he desired continued to leave him unsatisfied. Augustine compares himself to the prodigal son as he reflects writing:

"I have sought your face, O Lord, your face will I seek, for at that time I was far away from your countenance in darkness of spirit. Not with our feet or by traversing great distances do we journey away from you or find our way back. That younger son of yours in the gospel did not hire horses or carriages, nor did he board ships, nor take wing in any visible sense nor put one foot before the other when he journeyed to that far country where he could squander at will the wealth you, his gentle father, had given him at his departure. Gentle you were then, but gentler still with him when he returned in his need. No, to be estranged in a spirit of lust, and lost in its darkness, that is what it means to be far away from your face."[2]

The world of ancient Carthage, where Augustine sought his education, leads him further away from truth with various temptations to satisfy both carnally and intellectually. He explains:

"I was inwardly starved of that food which is yourself, O my God. Yet this inner famine created no pangs of hunger in me."[3]

Amid Augustine's famine, there was no ache to seek the Lord; he just sunk deeper into worldly satisfactions. Spellbound by theatrical shows that ignited great sorrow and a fixation on lust, his real-life actions reflected these stories. He enjoyed the feeling of grief brought on by the drama.

"At that time I was truly miserable, for I loved feeling sad and sought whatever could cause me sadness… I was an unhappy beast astray from your flock [Lord] and resentful of your shepherding, so what wonder was it that I became infected with foul mange?"[4]

Toxic friendships and the pursuit of earthly praise enable more deception. Augustine longed for wisdom and stumbled into the Manichaeism, a popular religion at that time.

Augustine's beliefs as a Manichee share similarities to some beliefs today. Although Manichees believed in God, they thought everything possessed a piece of God. They relied heavily on astrology and the view that stars predicted a person's behaviors and events.

Mani, the religion's founder, had expounded that he possessed the Holy Spirit in him and was leading others toward "holiness" through special knowledge. In many ways, it was a gnostic heresy, a perversion of Christianity. The religion encouraged the hierarchy of an "elect" who lived an ascetic lifestyle of virtues. Then there were the lower Manichees, or "hearers," that serviced them with works and alms. They didn't believe Jesus had an earthly body but was only a spirit.

> "I was hungering for you, but their teachings were like plates on which they served me not you, but the sun and moon, which are your beautiful works, to be sure, but still your works, not yourself, and not even your primary works at that."[5]

Augustine's main pursuit as a Manichee was determining the origins of evil and whether God possessed a body. The Manichee's belief that all creation contained God led to the absurd assertion that fruit held spiritual properties. If the Manichee elect consumed the fruit, they would emit divine particles when they exhaled. The lower rung of followers would sit faithfully by the elect, hoping to partake in these particles when the elect breathed out.

Even though Augustine was deceived by these matters, he still drew lines around situations he felt were outright demonic. He rebuffed efforts from others he knew crossed a moral line. In the case of a poetry contest he entered where a sorcerer offered to sacrifice animals on his behalf, Augustine refused the gesture.

> "Yet while refusing to have sacrifice offered to demons on my behalf I was all the while offering myself in sacrifice to them through my superstition."[6]

Augustine regrets how he remained in this folly for so long and the damage he was doing to his soul. Monica, his mother, regarded him "as dead"[7] due to these beliefs, weeping for her son bitterly.

At ages twenty-six and twenty-seven, Augustine authors a few books filled with Manichee philosophies on the existence of God, the nature of the world, and evil.

> "I babbled away in my petulant fashion asking 'If God made the soul, why does it fall into error.'.. I was readier to assert that you immutable substance had been forced into error than to confess that my own mutable substance had gone astray by its own will and that its error was its punishment."[8]

The deeper he immersed himself in the Manichee religion, Augustine found inconsistencies, conflicting beliefs, and unproven assertions. As he would press others on these things, they would either dismiss it or redirect him to inquire with a more elect Manichee. Finally, Augustine gets his chance and has the opportunity to meet one of the most admired Manichees, Faustus.

In meeting this admired man, Augustine finds him unimpressive. The celebrated Manichee is unable to answer his questions or explain the conflicting concepts. Augustine resolves Faustus's admiration among the Manichees was not because of some special knowledge or truth but the way he expressed it and his "handsome face and a graceful turn of speech."[9]

This pivotal moment in his life as a Manichee discourages Augustine. He realizes the religion does not hold perfect truth and begins to doubt whether truth can be known at all. Reflecting on this memory of false doctrine masquerading as truth, Augustine writes:

"I had already learned under your tuition [God] that nothing should be regarded as true because it is eloquently stated, nor false because the words sound clumsy. On the other hand, it is not true for being expressed in uncouth language either, nor false because couched in splendid words. I had come to understand that just as wholesome and rubbishy food may both be served equally well in sophisticated dishes or in others of rustic quality, so too can wisdom and foolishness be proffered in language elegant or plain."[10]

Augustine remains in famine, having no better place to go despite his dissatisfaction. This in-between space creates a conundrum for him as a teacher of rhetoric, where he finds himself lying, reciting the words people want to hear, words he no longer believed.

A poignant moment that brings him face-to-face with his deep unhappiness is when Augustine and his friends encounter a beggar in Milan. Augustine, anxious and consumed by unease, is preparing to give a eulogy for the emperor. Walking into town, they notice a beggar drunk and especially happy. Augustine makes fun of the beggar, but in doing so registers his own state worth ridicule. The beggar's joy is a feeling Augustine himself is tirelessly attempting to attain.

"With the help of the few paltry coins he had collected by begging, this man was enjoying the temporal happiness for which I strove by so bitter, devious and roundabout a contrivance. His joy was no true joy, to be sure, but what I was seeking in my ambition was a joy far more unreal; and he was undeniably happy while I was full of foreboding: he was carefree, I apprehensive."[11]

Augustine sees, in some ways, he is worse than the beggar. Albeit both are lacking, the efforts of his pursuits to bring him happiness were failing him. The beggar had found a temporal joy that was, at the moment, better than Augustine's state of being.

Even still, Augustine admits,

"asking whether I preferred to be like the beggar, or to be as I was then. I would have chosen to be myself, laden with anxieties and fears. Surely that would have been no right choice, but a perverse one? I could not have preferred my condition to his on the grounds that I was better educated, because that fact was not for me a source of joy but only the means by which I sought to curry favor with human beings: I was not aiming to teach them but only to win their favor."[12]

The beggar was enjoying his drunkenness, while Augustine was miserable in his desire for glory. In his disobedient state, Augustine writes he was just as intoxicated with errant things.

"[The beggar] would sleep off his intoxication that same night, whereas I had slept with mine and risen up again, and would sleep and rise with it again."[13]

QUESTIONS

1. What are the needs Augustine is trying to fill during this time?

2. Where did Augustine turn in order to fill those needs?

3. How does Augustine describe his unhappiness during this period of life?

4. What ways do people satisfy their needs today?

5. Where do you find yourself feeling a sense of famine or unfulfilled need?

6. What areas of your life need to be handed over to God so he can satisfy?

"The young man said to him, 'I have kept all these; what do I still lack?' Jesus said to him, 'If you wish to be perfect, go, sell your possessions, and give the money to the poor, and you will have treasure in heaven; then come, follow me.'"

MATTHEW 19:20-22 (NRSV)

Image: Ruins of ancient Carthage. Credit: R.maabid, CC BY-SA 4.0, via Wikimedia Commons

Rest

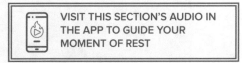
VISIT THIS SECTION'S AUDIO IN THE APP TO GUIDE YOUR MOMENT OF REST

As you finish this part of the study, visit the mobile app for this section's Rest meditation song. Additionally, below is an excerpt from Augustine's *Confessions* in which he implores the Lord to cleanse his soul .

THE HOUSE OF MY SOUL

The house of my soul is too small for you to enter: make it more spacious by your coming.

It lies in ruins: rebuild it.

Some things are to be found there which will offend your gaze; I confess this to be so and know it well.

But who will clean my house?

To whom but yourself can I cry, "Cleanse me of my hidden sins, O Lord, and for those incurred through others pardon your servant?"

I believe, and so I will speak.

"You know everything, Lord."

Have I not laid my own transgressions bare before you to my own condemnation, my God, and have you not forgiven the wickedness of my heart? I do not argue my case against you, for you are truth itself; nor do I wish to deceive myself, lest my iniquity be caught in its own lies."

No, I do not argue the case with you, because if you, Lord, keep the score of our iniquities, then who, Lord, can bear it?

- St. Augustine of Hippo,
***The Confessions*, Book I,**
Section 6

PART 3 - SHEPHERD'S VOICE

Image: View of Wadi Qelt, Israel thought to be the Valley of the Shadow in Psalm 23 and where the parable of the Good Samaritan is set.

PART 3

Shepherd's Voice

> "How many of my father's hired hands have bread enough and to spare, but here I am dying of hunger! I will get up and go to my father..."

LUKE 15:17-18 (NRSV)

Image: Jesus' empty tomb in the Church of the Holy Sepulchre, Jerusalem, Israel

Read

DEEP DIVE INTO SCRIPTURE

Read Luke 15:15-19 "So he went and hired himself out to one of the citizens of that country, who sent him to his fields to feed the pigs…" As you dig into verses 15-19, let's explore supporting verses from both the Old and New Testaments that use the Greek word for the action the son takes "to get up"(*anistēmi*). Using your Bible, write out the verses noting any differences in your translation.

Word / Phrase	Verse	Write Out His Word
get up, arise, stand, establish, raise up (English) anistēmi (Greek)	Psalm 41:10	
	Job 1:20	
	Isaiah 11:10	
	Ephesians 5:14	
	1 Thessalonians 4:16	

TO RISE UP

The prodigal son's moment of realization explained in the verses as his "coming to himself," is followed by the Greek word *anistēmi*, to arise or get up. This word carries significant weight when examining its usage in the context of the New Testament. It conveys physical movement and spiritual implications, representing a restoration and establishment of oneself.

It is worth noting, too, that just before he mentions that he will "arise," he first states that he is "dying." The word used for dying in this passage is *apollymi*, the same Greek word used in the first part of our study for lost. Note the repetition of the word throughout all these verses, like a drumbeat through the parable.

The Greek word *anistēmi* (pronounced an-is'-tay-mee) means "to get up, arise, raise up, rise again, to establish oneself."[1] It's a simple movement and a common word. However, viewing it in the context of scripture, there are some beautiful parallels between the action and the son coming back to life.

anistēmi - arise, rise up, rise again, raise up, stand up

In the Psalms, King David employs the word *anistēmi* when speaking of his redemption, pleading for God's grace.

> "But you, O Lord, be gracious to me, and raise me up (*anistēmi*), that I may repay them." Psalm 41:10

Here, the word implies a desire to be lifted out of a state of distress and brokenness, highlighting the parallel with the prodigal son's journey back to his father.

The book of Job is a profound exploration of human suffering and the sovereignty of God. Job, a righteous and blameless man, experiences unimaginable loss, including the deaths of his children and the affliction of his own body. Despite his anguish, Job remains faithful to God and refuses to curse Him. After news that he has lost everything he has, the passage states:

> "Then Job arose (*anistēmi*), tore his robe, shaved his head, and fell on the ground and worshiped." Job 1:20

Job's response to his devastating circumstances is to be admired. Instead of succumbing to despair, he arises, only to then tear his robe and fall on the ground to worship God. Using the word *anistēmi* before Job falls to the ground demonstrates his humility. It signifies the word as a spiritual shift, a change from one state to another.

The verse's use of the word implies a similar action to the son in the parable, a response to a terrible realization. While Job arises to then fall on the ground to worship the Lord, the son arises to run home to the father.

Throughout the Greek Old Testament, *anistēmi* is used in the context of being joined in glory with the Lord, receiving redemption and new life. The prophet Isaiah ministered during a time of political turmoil and spiritual decline in Israel. In Isaiah 11, the prophet delivers a message of hope and peace to the people of Israel.

> "On that day the root of Jesse shall stand (*anistēmi*) as a signal to the peoples; the nations shall inquire of him, and his dwelling shall be glorious." Isaiah 11:10

Isaiah foretells the day God will restore them with the coming of the Messiah. It's a prophetic proclamation of His redemptive plan and His desire to bring His people into a season of rest.

In the Old Testament, "raising up" prophets are also described using the word *anistēmi*. Moses addresses the new generation of Israelites, reminding them of God's covenant and laws.

> "The Lord your God will raise up (*anistēmi*) for you a prophet like me from among your own people; you shall heed such a prophet." Deuteronomy 18:15

This prophecy anticipates the coming of Jesus Christ, who fulfills the role of the ultimate prophet, teacher, guide, and redeemer of humanity.

The New Testament employs *anistēmi* 112 times, both literally and figuratively. Throughout the Gospels, Jesus speaks about raising believers on the last day, so much so, that it confuses Martha when Jesus says her brother Lazarus will rise from the dead.

> "Jesus said to her, 'Your brother will rise (*anistēmi*) again.' Martha said to him, 'I know that he will rise again in the resurrection on the last day.' Jesus said to her, 'I am the resurrection and the life. Those who believe in me, even though they die, will live, and everyone who lives and believes in me will never die. Do you believe this?" John 11:23-26

All throughout Jesus' teachings he emphasizes the spiritual awakening and restoration that occurs through Him. Even still the disciples cannot decipher the spiritual from the physical as recorded in in the Gospel of John when it says:

> "Then the other disciple, who reached the tomb first, also went in, and he saw and believed; for as yet they did not understand the scripture, that he must rise (*anistēmi*) from the dead." John:8-9

Jesus' mission is to reconcile humanity to God. He accomplishes this through His sacrificial death and resurrection.

The prodigal son's arising is not solely a physical awakening from a desperate situation but also a profound spiritual transformation. The apostle Paul writes to the Ephesians emphasizing the need for spiritual awakening and conversion:

> "For it is shameful even to mention what such people do secretly; but everything exposed by the light becomes visible, for everything that becomes visible is light. Therefore it says, 'Sleeper, awake! Rise (*anistēmi*) from the dead, and Christ will shine on you.'" Ephesians 5:14

To the Thessalonians Paul reassures that at the return of Christ, the dead will rise.

> "For the Lord himself, with a cry of command, with the archangel's call and with the sound of God's trumpet, will descend from heaven, and the dead in Christ will rise (*anistēmi*) first." 1 Thessalonians 4:16

In the parable, the son's physical movement as he arises from the pigsty carries deep spiritual significance. *Anistēmi* encompasses a visual, connecting with various scriptural verses from the Old and New Testaments. It emphasizes a key moment in the prodigal son's journey of redemption and restoration, highlighting the transformative power of God's grace and gift of eternal life.

Reflect

on the app...

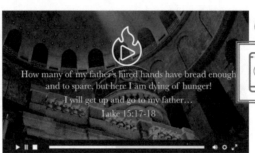

How many of my father's hired hands have bread enough and to spare, but here I am dying of hunger! I will get up and go to my father...

Luke 15:17-18

VISIT THIS SECTION'S MEDITATION VIDEO IN THE APP FOR A MOMENT OF GUIDED REFLECTION

REFLECTION FROM AN EARLY CHURCH FATHER

" When a man's love then goes even away from himself to those things which are without, he begins to share the vanity of his vain desires, and prodigal as it were to spend his strength. He is dissipated, exhausted, without resource or strength, he feeds swine; and wearied with this office of feeding swine, he at last remembers what he was, and says, "How many hired servants of my Father's are eating bread, and I here perish with hunger!" But when the son in the parable says this, what is said of him, who had squandered all he had on harlots, who wished to have in his own power what was being well kept for him with his father..? "... when he returned to himself."

If "he returned to himself," he had gone away from himself. Because he had fallen from himself,... he returns first to himself, that he may return to that state from which he had fallen away by falling from himself.... Returning then to himself, that he might not remain in himself, what did he say? "I will arise and go to my Father."

See, whence he had fallen away from himself, he had fallen away from his Father; he had fallen away from himself, he had gone away from himself to those things which are without. He returns to himself, and goes to his Father, where he may keep himself in all security... Let him not trust in himself, let him feel that he is a man, and have respect to the words of the prophet, "Cursed is every one that puts his hope in man." ... Let him withdraw himself from himself, that he may cleave unto God. Whatever of good he has, let him commit to Him by whom he was made; whatever of evil he has, he has made it for himself. The evil that is in him God made not; let him destroy what himself has done, who has been thereby undone. "Let him deny himself," He says, "and take up his cross, and follow Me."

- St. Augustine of Hippo, *Sermon 46 on the New Testament* (393-430 AD)

As you ponder these verses, journal your thoughts in the space provided. Reflect on the scripture passage (and subsequent supporting passages) from "Read." Is there a word that stands out? What do these verses mean to you? What is the Holy Spirit showing you in these scripture passages?

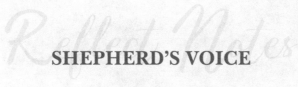

SHEPHERD'S VOICE

Image: Entrance to the church built in the fourth century by Saint Ambrose. Basilica of St. Ambrose, Milan, Italy

Respond

In this section, we will continue our look at Augustine of Hippo, and his response to God's word. May it serve as example as you seek out how the Holy Spirit is prompting you to Respond.

RESPONDING TO HIS VOICE

From the moment Augustine dives into sinful spiritual deception, there is a shift in the narrative of his mother, Monica. Where once she was occupied by his education and career success, her concern morphs into worry for the salvation of her son's soul. Augustine notes that although his mother's objections came from her mouth, they were not her's alone.

"By using her you [Lord] were not silent to me."[2]

Monica echoes the shepherd's voice in her son's life. In his adolescent years, they were warnings to avoid sexual relationships with women. Then they evolve to more profound anguish as she opposes the deception of his Manichaeism thinking. It appears Augustine never relented or showed signs of heeding her advice since he writes that his mother regarded him as dead.

In her constant tears and prayers, the Lord is gracious to Monica and gives her a vision.

"She dreamt that she was standing on some kind of a wooden ruler, and saw a young man of radiant aspect coming toward her."[3]

She was overwhelmed with grief in the dream, yet the man was cheerful. The man asks her why she is crying, to which she replies that she is mourning the death of her son.

"He then instructed her to take good heed and see that where she stood, there I stood also."[4]

In telling her son her dream, she explains to Augustine that he was next to her in the same place on the wooden ruler. In his pride, he laughs, stating that this must mean she was to ascend to his lofty position of heightened enlightenment. However, Monica knew what she saw and continued her prayers with hope, having been assured by the Lord her son would arise.

Augustine remembers that although he laughed, this dream from his mother disturbed him. In sharing it, his mother had rattled something inside him. Yet, it would still be another nine years in which he would "flounder in the mud of the deep and the darkness of deception."[5]

Augustine sees the good shepherd's voice as coming through many people, even those that did not follow Christ. One example is that of a man who convinced him of the folly of astrology. A skilled doctor with deep insight shared with Augustine that he, too, had been deceived and that astrology was entirely misleading.

"By the answer he gave me, or which you [Lord] gave me through him, you made provision for my needs and

sketched in my memory an outline of
the truth I was later to search out for
myself."[6]

Augustine recalls another example of
God's voice in his life from a dear friend
before that friend's untimely death. While
the friend was unconscious with illness, he
was baptized.

On hearing this, Augustine teases his
recovering friend for the absurdity of being
baptized at all. The friend, whom
Augustine believed to be in the same
mindset as him, is upset by the remark.

"He recoiled of me with a shudder as
though I had been his enemy. Warned
me that if I wished to be his friend, I
had better stop saying such things."[7]

Augustine didn't know what to do with this,
and before there was much to say, his dear
friend died a few days later. This event
threw Augustine into tremendous grief.

"I had become a great enigma to
myself, and I questioned my soul,
demanding why it was sorrowful and
why it so disquieted me."[8]

Not only did Augustine believe that the
Lord reached out to him through others,
but also used external circumstances like
the change of career to position a change
of heart. He reflects on this when recalling
his move from Carthage to Rome, a
significant relocation in the 4th century.

"But in truth, it was you, my hope and
my inheritance in the country of the
living, who for my soul's salvation
prompted me to change my country,
and to this end, you provided both the
goads at Carthage that dislodged me
from there and the allurements at
Rome that attracted me;"[9]

This move completely devastates Monica,
and she tries to convince him to stay. Yet
Augustine states the Lord "took no heed in
her requests" to stop him as this move was
pivotal to "making me into what she was
asking for all the time."[10]

In Rome, Augustine officially decides to
stop trying to make sense of the
Manichaeism.

"By now I had given up hope of
making any progress in that false
doctrine, so I held onto the teaching
half-heartedly and without giving them
much thought simply because I had
resolved to make do with them in
default of anything better."[11]

Through his success and position in Rome,
Augustine receives the opportunity to be a
master of rhetoric in Milan. It is a
considerable advancement in his career.
Milan, Italy, in the 4th century, was the
center of government since it was where
the Western emperor resided. While the
opportunity is for his career, Augustine
admits he took the position "to get away
from the Manichees."[12]

Awaiting him in Milan is a great orator
that would change his life forever. Through
his love of eloquence and words Augustine
had been curious to meet, a bishop named
Ambrose. He has heard him spoken of
highly and wanted to see the gift for
himself.

"This man of God welcomed me with
fatherly kindness and showed the
charitable concern for my pilgrimage
that befitted a bishop. I began to feel
affection for him, not at first as a
teacher of truth, for that I had given up
hope of finding in your Church, but
simply as a man who was kind to me.
With professional interest I listened to

him conducting disputes before the people, but my intention was not the right one: was assessing his eloquence to see whether it matched its reputation. I wished to ascertain whether the readiness of speech with which rumor credited him was really there, or something more, or less. I hung keenly upon his words, but cared little for their content, and indeed despised it, as I stood there delighting in the sweetness of his discourse."[13]

As Augustine recalls this move from Rome to Milan, he is confident that the Lord's intended to use Ambrose to reach him.

"Little by little, without knowing it, I was drawing near."[14]

Ambrose's homilies impacted Augustine in understanding the Old Testament, which seemed confusing and less intellectually exciting than his Manichean philosophies.

"I realized that the Catholic faith, in support of which I had believed nothing could be advanced against the Manichean opponents was in fact intellectually respectable."[15]

Augustine had yet to encounter anyone like Ambrose. He was accessible but read quietly in solitude, to which Augustine hesitates to interrupt in order to seek answers. This small detail is important as it encourages Augustine to rely on understanding scripture for his answers, not unique artful words from a great speaker.

Through Ambrose, Augustine hears the shepherd's voice in its fullness and is curious about the truth initially hidden from him behind misconceptions.

"I resolved, therefore, to live as a catechumen in the Catholic Church, which was what my parents had wished for me, until some kind of certainty dawned by which I might direct my steps aright."[16]

Upon hearing this, his mother, Monica, rejoices that her prayers and promises are being fulfilled. She boards a boat to Milan to live with her son. Augustine was yet a Catholic Christian, but even his sincere interest and disavowing of Manichaeism were enough for her to be overjoyed.

Monica is so confident of Augustine's eventual conversion that on her perilous journey, she boldly assures the sailors they won't die and will go safely to port because of her dream from the Lord.

After years of prayers, Monica finally glimpses the impossible–her son arising, awakening to the truth.

"She would cry over me who though dead could still be raised to life again; she offered me to you [Lord] upon the bier of her meditation begging you to say … 'Young man, arise, I tell you.'" [17]

Indeed Augustine had arisen, just like the prodigal son "coming to himself." He resolves to know what scripture holds for him, ingest the words of Ambrose, and welcome the prayers of his faithful mother.

QUESTIONS

1. In what ways did Augustine hear God's voice?

2. What did Monica hope for son and what convinced her?

3. In what ways can you say Augustine arose out of his deception?

4. How does this world make it difficult to hear God's voice?

5. What circumstances has God used to move you out of deception?

6. Are there any ways you feel you are God's voice to others?

"But you, O Lord, be gracious to me, and raise me up, that I may repay them.."

PSALM 41:10

Image: View overlooking the red sand desert th[...]
Israelites wandered. Wadi Rum, Jordan

Rest

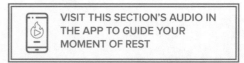

VISIT THIS SECTION'S AUDIO IN
THE APP TO GUIDE YOUR
MOMENT OF REST

As you finish this part of the study, visit the mobile app for this section's Rest meditation song. Additionally, below is an excerpt from Augustine's *Confessions*, a beautiful exposition on the Lord calling him back.

LATE HAVE I LOVED YOU

Late have I loved you, Beauty so ancient and so new, late have I loved you!

Lo, you were within, but I outside, seeking there for you, and upon the shapely things you have made I rushed headlong.

I, misshapen. You were with me, but I was not with you. They held me back far from you, those things which would have no being were they not in you.

You called, shouted, broke through my deafness; you flared, blazed, banished my blindness; you lavished your fragrance, I gasped, and now I pant for you; I tasted you, and I hunger and thirst; you touched me, and I burned for your peace.

When at last I cling to you with my whole being there will be no more anguish or labor for me, and my life will be alive indeed, because filled with you.

**- St. Augustine of Hippo,
The Confessions, Book X,
Section 38**

PART 4 - COMING HOME

Image: The ruins of ancient Hippo and St. Augustine Basilica, Annaba, Algeria. Credit: Kris Hellstrom, Director ASA Cultural Tours.

PART 4

Coming Home

WILL ARISE AND
GO TO MY FATHER

HE SAW HIM AND
HAD COMPASSION

> *But while he was still far off, his father saw him and was filled with compassion; he ran and put his arms around him and kissed him.*
>
> **LUKE 15:20 (NRSV)**

Read

DEEP DIVE INTO SCRIPTURE

R ead Luke 15:20-21 "So he set off and went to his father. But while he was still far off, his father saw him and was filled with compassion; he ran and put his arms around him and kissed him…" To gain deeper understanding of verses 20-21, let's explore supporting verses from both the Old and New Testaments that share the same keyword of compassion or *splagchnizomai* in Greek. To begin, look up these verses below in the Bible (your preferred translation) and write them out in the space provided.

Word / Phrase	Verse	Write Out His Word
feel sympathy, to pity, to have or be moved with compassion (English) splagchnizomai (Greek)	Zechariah 12:10	
	2 Chronicles 30:9	
	Matthew 9:36	
	Luke 7:13	
	Luke 10:33	

TO BE MOVED

The Greek word used in Luke 15 to describe the compassion of the father, *splagchnizomai*, carries a unique and powerful meaning. It signifies compassion that is not limited to a mere feeling of the heart or mind but is felt deep within the bowels, invoking a physical response.

Splagchnizomai (pronounced splawk-nidz-zo-mah) is used 17 times in the Greek New Testament and is sometimes translated as "moved"[1] when not rendered as compassion.

splagchnizomai - compassion, pity, to be moved

When the Gospel writers narrate Jesus' compassion, they often employs this precise word. For example, in Matthew, it says:

> "When he saw the crowds, he had compassion (*splagchnizomai*) for them because they were harassed and helpless, like sheep without a shepherd." Matthew 9:36

The Gospel writer Luke uses it to describe Christ's deep emotion when a widow lost her son who was visibly dead.

> "When the Lord saw her, he had compassion (*splagchnizomai*) for her and said to her, 'Do not weep.' Then he came forward and touched the bier, and the bearers stood still. And he said, 'Young man, I say to you, rise!' The dead man sat up and began to speak, and Jesus gave him to his mother." Luke 7:13-15

Imagine how the widow must have looked or sounded to move the Lord to such compassion. Being a widow, we can safely assume this boy was all she had. Jesus performs a major public miracle raising the boy from the dead. Carrying out this miracle, he says "rise" or *anistēmi*, the same Greek word from the previous section.

The Gospel writer Luke again uses *splagchnizomai* when communicating the Parable of the Good Samaritan in Luke chapter 10. Upon seeing the wounded man, the Samaritan is profoundly moved with compassion, compelling him to act and provide assistance.

> "But a Samaritan while traveling came near him; and when he saw him, he was moved with pity (*splagchnizomai*)." Luke 10:33

The good samaritan felt compassion physically. It resonated deep inside of him. To not act would have been contrary to his whole being.

In the Greek Old Testament, *splagchnizomai* is not directly applied to God, as He does not possess a physical body. Instead, the closest Greek word used for compassion is *oiktirmos* (pronounced oyk-tir-mos).[2] Through this word, we gain insight into God's compassion in the Old Testament and how it aligns with the compassion that Jesus speaks of.

The 2nd book of Chronicles offers a glimpse of God's compassion on His people. The verse assures that their children will find compassion when returning to Him, thus foreshadowing Jesus' parable.

> "For as you return to the Lord, your kindred and your children will find compassion (*oiktirmos*) with their captors, and return to this land. For the Lord your God is gracious and

merciful, and will not turn away his face from you, if you return to him." 2 Chronicles 30:9

Although this parallels the compassionate father in Jesus's parable, in Christ's story, the father runs toward the lost while they are still on the road. That is only possible because of Jesus, the one who clears the way home to the heavenly Father.

In the book of Zechariah, a prophecy foretells the compassion that will flow from Jesus' sacrificial death on the cross.

> "And I will pour out a spirit of compassion (*oiktirmos*) and supplication on the house of David and the inhabitants of Jerusalem, so that, when they look on the one whom they have pierced, they shall mourn for him, as one mourns for an only child, and weep bitterly over him, as one weeps over a firstborn." Zechariah 12:10

Throughout the Old Testament, God's compassion is evident, frequently expressed in the Psalms and witnessed in the story of Israel as a people who often stray but return to God.

Psalm 51, authored by King David, is a powerful and heartfelt expression of repentance and seeking God's forgiveness.

David composed this psalm after being confronted by the prophet Nathan for his adulterous affair with Bathsheba and his guilt in the death of her husband, Uriah. The Psalm is a passionate plea for God's mercy and compassion, acknowledging the gravity of David's transgressions and his deep desire for spiritual renewal and restoration.

> "Have mercy (*oiktirmos*) on me, O God, according to your steadfast love;

according to your abundant mercy blot out my transgressions. Wash me thoroughly from my iniquity, and cleanse me from my sin." Psalm 51:1-2

In 1 Kings 8, the author (often attributed to the prophet Jeremiah) recounts the grand dedication of the temple built by King Solomon in Jerusalem. This momentous occasion marks the fulfillment of David's desire to construct a permanent dwelling place for the Lord. The chapter documents Solomon's prayer of dedication, in which he appeals to God for mercy, forgiveness, and compassion.

> "and forgive your people who have sinned against you, and all their transgressions that they have committed against you; and grant them compassion (*oiktirmos*) in the sight of their captors, so that they may have compassion on them." 1 Kings 8:50

Christ's sacrificial death firmly establishes an assurance of finding compassion upon returning to God. As Christ bears our sins, He paves the path of return, portraying the heavenly Father as one who runs towards us on the road, eagerly willing to carry us the rest of the way.

Understanding that Christ, in His fully human nature, physically felt compassion should encourage us of His love. It should also provoke us to extend compassion to others, united in the expressive power of *splagchnizomai*, which touches us at our core and moves us to act.

Reflect

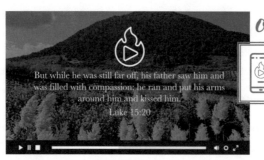

But while he was still far off, his father saw him and was filled with compassion; he ran and put his arms around him and kissed him.
Luke 15:20

on the app...

VISIT THIS SECTION'S MEDITATION VIDEO IN THE APP FOR A MOMENT OF GUIDED REFLECTION

REFLECTION FROM AN EARLY CHURCH FATHER

" The father, you see, made no delay in being reconciled. Our heavenly Father is only too willing to be reconciled, when we ask Him in earnest. So let us learn by what approach we should seek pardon from the Father. Listen to the son's words: "'Father', he says" (Lk 15:21). What forgiveness, what tenderness we see in one who, no matter how hurt he had been by his child, does not forbid him to call him 'father!' 'Father,' he says, 'I have sinned against Heaven and before you.'"(Lk 15:21).

Such is his first avowal to him who is the author of his life, the master of mercy, the judge of his sin. True, God knows all things, but all the same He likes to hear the expression of our sorrow and regret. For "with the mouth confession is made for our justification" (Rm 10:10). By confessing one lightens the weight of one's sin; and by owning up in advance one takes the sting out of the accusation; for "the just person begins by accusing himself (Pr 18.17)..."

Have no fear of not being heard. The advocate guarantees your pardon; the patron promises you forgiveness; your defender assures you, with fatherly kindness, that you are reconciled. Believe, for He is all truth; be at peace, for He is your strength. It is in the interests of Christ to intercede for you, because for your sake He died. He does not want His death to be in vain. The Father also has reason to forgive, for whatever the Son wants, He wants too...

- St. Ambrose, *Exposition on the Gospel of St. Luke*, Book VII (377 AD)

As you ponder these verses, journal your thoughts in the space provided. Reflect on the scripture passage (and subsequent supporting passages) from "Read." Is there a word that stands out? What do these verses mean to you? What is the Holy Spirit showing you in these scripture passages?

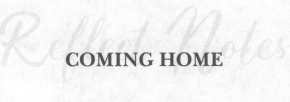

COMING HOME

Image: The villa where Augustine lived at the
time of his conversion. Rus Cassiciacum,
Cassago Brianza, Italy

Respond

ON THE JOURNEY HOME

In this section, we will continue our look at Augustine of Hippo, and his response to God's word. May it serve as example as you seek out how the Holy Spirit is prompting you to Respond.

In Augustine's "arise" moment, he commits to learning about the faith. Studying God through Christian beliefs sets him on a challenging road filled with intellectual and emotional setbacks.

"I was full of doubts about all these things and scarcely believed it possible to find the way of life."[3]

Bishop Ambrose helps make scripture understandable, allowing Augustine to break free from the deceitful fallacies told to him and eventually find the truth. He had become so conditioned in his previous way of thinking that the first breakthrough was his realization of what the Christian church actually taught.

"I had been arguing blindly in the objections I raised against your Catholic Church. I had not yet come to accept her teachings as true, but at least I now knew that she did not teach the doctrines to which I had gravely objected."[4]

Much like the prodigal son who believes he can only return to the father as a hired servant, Augustine makes his way to the Lord unaware of the fullness of mercy offered. He struggles to understand the nature of God and his place in it all.

"... just as someone who has suffered under a bad physician may often be afraid to entrust himself to a good one,

so it was in my soul's case."[5]

At this time Augustine is assured of a few truths, that God exists, He cares, and He is all good. Yet, Augustine struggles with the nature of sin, its existence, and how sin and evil could exist in a world of a good God. This becomes an intellectual battle for Augustine. In retrospect, he writes:

"All the while, Lord, as I pondered these things you stood by me; I sighed and you heard me; I was tossed to and fro and you steered me aright. I wandered down the wide road of the world, but you did not desert me."[6]

Even still, the fullness of God's truth was not coming fast enough.

"Here I was in my thirtieth year sticking fast in the same muddy bog… 'Tomorrow,' I had been saying to myself, 'tomorrow I will find it; it will appear plainly, and I will grasp it."[7]

Augustine's delay wasn't intellectual, it was from his own resistance to reject sin.

"I put off being converted to the Lord and from day to day pushed away from me the day when I would live in you, though I could not postpone a daily dying in myself. Though I was so enamored of a happy life, I feared to find it in its true home, and fled from it even as I sought it. For I thought I would be exceedingly miserable if deprived of a woman's embrace, and gave no thought to the medicine prepared by your mercy for the healing of this infirmity."[8]

Seeing the hold of lust on Augustine, his mother, Monica, prepares a marriage for him. She insists he end the ongoing relationship of fourteen years with the mother of Augustine's son Adeodatus. He obeys despite it immediately inflicting a wound in his heart. The agony of relinquishing this woman spins Augustine into more sin to satisfy the hurt. The pain, however, pulls him back to himself.

"Already your right hand [Lord] was ready to seize me and pull me out of the filth, yet did I not know it. The only thing that restrained me from being sucked still deeper into the whirlpool of carnal lusts was the fear of death and of your future judgment."[9]

As Augustine draws closer to God, his intellectual journey evolves into a struggle of satisfaction. He wants to be convinced that God will satisfy him should he abandon his lusts and desire for glory.

The prodigal son also must have doubted what life in his father's house would look like, what a hired servant's life would offer him, and even if the father would accept his return.

Yet, unlike the prodigal son, who physically did not have much to leave behind, Augustine was rich in worldly accomplishments. Although Augustine lets go of Manicheaism, and astrology, the big hurdle of lust continues to have a pull on him.

"I was drawn toward you [Lord] by your beauty but swiftly dragged away from you by my own weight, swept back headlong and groaning onto these things below myself."[10]

It is then that Augustine is led to the writings of Paul in the New Testament and discovers the reason for his difficulty understanding God. He had completely missed the significance of Jesus Christ.

"Accordingly, I looked for a way to gain the strength I needed to enjoy you, but I did not find it until I embraced the mediator between God and humankind, the man Christ Jesus."[11]

On the road back to the heavenly Father, he realizes that the one helping him out of the muddy bog, past the hurdle of astrology, clearing the paths of temptation along the way, has been Christ, the Good Shepherd, the whole time. Through the writings of Paul's letters, Augustine discovers the mercy and grace of God and a burden lifts.

"What is a human wretch to do? Who will free him from this death-laden body, if not your grace, given through Jesus Christ our Lord… In him the ruler of this world found nothing that deserved death, yet slew him all the same; and so the record of debt that stood against us was annulled."[12]

This point in Augustine's journey marks a shift, a breath of fresh air, as he leans on Christ to complete the pilgrimage home. One new obstacle emerges, however, the nature of his profession.

"I was irked by the secular business I was conducting, for no longer was I fired by ambition, and prepared on that account to endure such heavy servitude in hope of reputation and wealth, as had formerly been the case. Those prospects held no charm for me now…"[13]

Although it was lawful that Augustine could be a Christian and a teacher of rhetoric, Augustine knew he could not in good conscience do both. He fights against this as if it were two wills inside of him.

> "A new will had begun to emerge in me, the will to worship you disinterestedly and enjoy you, oh God… I had grown used to pretending that the only reason why I had not yet turned my back on the world to serve you was that my perceptions of the truth was uncertain, but that excuse was no longer available to me, for by now I was certain."[14]

During this struggle, the Lord sends a stranger, Ponticianus, to visit Augustine, asking for a favor in travel to Northern Africa. It comes to Augustine's attention that he is also a Christian. In Ponticianus's enthusiasm, he shares the story of a close friend who renounced the world for a life of solitude and prayer. It is the first time Augustine learns of ascetic life and St. Antony of the Desert, the originator of the practice.

> "There [his friend] found a book which contained The Life of Antony… and as he read he began to mull over the possibility of appropriating the same kind of life for himself, by renouncing his secular career to serve you alone… He turned his gaze to his [companion] and demanded, 'Tell me: where do we hope our efforts are going to get us?… And how long would it take us to get there? Whereas I can become a friend of God here and now if I want to.'"[15]

This story from a stranger awakens a desire in Augustine and a profound conflict as he yearns for that prayerful lifestyle.

> "Ponticianus went on with his story; but, Lord, even while he spoke you were wrenching me back toward myself, and pulling me round from that standpoint behind my back which I had taken to avoid looking at myself."[16]

It's as if God's merciful rays reveal his sin so distinctly and clearly that Augustine can no longer look at the Father or himself. He is so disgusted by this realization that it causes to him to he fall into violent conflict.

> "All I knew was that I was going mad… I was groaning in spirit and shaken by violent anger because I could form no resolve to enter into a covenant with you, though in my bones I knew that this was what I ought to do."[17]

When the visitor leaves, Augustine runs outside to the garden. He weeps bitterly but stops when he hears a voice from a nearby house. It's a young child singing a simple song, "Pick it up and read, pick it up and read."[18] Having never heard this tune before, nor that voice, he takes it as a directive and heads back to the table where he had left a book from Paul's letter to the Romans.

> "I snatched it up, opened it and read in silence the passage which my eyes first lighted: *Not in dissipation and drunkenness, nor in debauchery and lewdness, nor in arguing and jealousy; but put on the Lord Jesus Christ, and make no provision for the flesh or the gratification of your desires.* I had no wish to read further, nor was there need. No sooner had I reached the end of the verse than the light of certainty flooded my heart and all dark shades of doubt fled away."[18]

QUESTIONS

1. What were the chief struggles Augustine had to overcome before conversion?

2. Why do you think Augustine's conversion could not remain solely intellectual?

3. What impact does Christ the mediator and redeemer have on Augustine's conversion?

4. What challenges of today's world get in the way of receiving God's merciful embrace?

5. What is the difference in intellectually understanding the faith and surrendering to it?

6. Is there anything you are holding back from surrendering to the Lord?

"When he saw the crowds, he had compassion for them, because they were harassed and helpless, like sheep without a shepherd."

MATTHEW 9:36 (NSRV)

Image: A field at the bottom of Mount Tabor, the site of the Transfiguration of Christ, in the region of Galilee, Israel

Rest

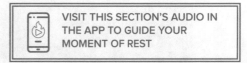

VISIT THIS SECTION'S AUDIO IN THE APP TO GUIDE YOUR MOMENT OF REST

As you finish this part of the study, visit the mobile app for this section's Rest meditation song. Additionally, below is an excerpt from Augustine's *Confessions* on the satisfaction of coming home.

OUR HOME IS YOUR ETERNITY

O Lord our God, grant us to trust in your overshadowing wings: protect us beneath them and bear us up.

You will carry us as little children, and even to our grey-headed age you will carry us still.

When you are our strong security, that is strength indeed, but when our security is in ourselves, that is but weakness.

Our good abides ever in your keeping, but in diverting our steps from you we have grown perverse.

Let us turn back to you at last, Lord, that we be not overturned. Unspoilt, our good abides with you, for you are yourself our good.

We need not fear to find no home again because we have fallen away from it; while we are absent our home falls not to ruins, for our home is your eternity.

-St. Augustine of Hippo, *The Confessions*, Book IV, Section 31

PART 5 - RRECONCILIATION

Image: View of the Jordan River in Northern
rael where baptisms occur daily

PART 5

Reconciliation

> " *... get the fatted calf and kill it, and let us eat and celebrate; for this son of mine was dead and is alive again; he was lost and is found!"*

LUKE 15:21 (NRSV)

Image: A sheep returning to the herd in Negev Heights near Revivim, Israel. Image by Micha Baranovsky, via Wikimedia Commons

Read

DEEP DIVE INTO SCRIPTURE

Read Luke 15:5, 15:9 and Luke 15:22-24 "...for this son of mine was dead and is alive again; he was lost and is found!" As you review verses 5, 9 and 22-24 of the study, compare them with the supporting verses from both the Old and New Testaments that also speak to "being found," the Greek word *heyriskō*. Looking up these verses below in your own Bible, write them down in the space provided along with any notes.

Word / Phrase	Verse	Write Out His Word
to find, to discover, to come upon, obtain (English) heyriskō (Greek)	Psalm 89:20	
	Isaiah 65:1	
	Jeremiah 29:13	
	Mathew 7:7	
	2 Peter 3:14	

SEEK AND YOU WILL FIND

English translations of scripture commonly lack the literary device of repetition. For a more agreeable literary style, modern English relies heavily on synonyms.

Yet, both the Greek and Hebrew texts of the Old and New Testament emphasize the significance of a word through repetition. Since scripture was initially intended to be recited orally, repetition reinforced the meaning of God's word to listeners and aided memory recall.

Repetition becomes a rhythmic drumbeat creating a musical quality in the text. Throughout the parable in Luke 15, is a rhythmic beat of lost *apollymi* and found *heyriskō*.[1] *Apollymi* is used seven times and *heyriskō* eight times.

Heyriskō, (pronounced hyoo-ris'-ko) appears over 175 times in the Greek New Testament.[1] The familiar Greek word "Eureka!" derives from *heyriskō* and translates to "I've found it!"

heyriskō - to discover, obtain, to find

Jesus addresses the discovery of the Kingdom of Heaven throughout the New Testament. He assures His disciples in Matthew 7:

> "Ask, and it will be given to you; search, and you will find (*heyriskō*); knock, and the door will be opened for you."
> Matthew 7:7

This verse reinforces the gracious giving of the father, who, after the son had squandered away his wealth, welcomed him back with a feast.

In the Old Testament King David's experiences reflect the pattern of feeling lost and subsequently found by God. The Psalms authored by David often express his heartfelt laments, vividly illustrating how the Lord finds him in moments of distress and how David, in turn, earnestly seeks the Lord.

In Psalm 89, David recalls the moment the Lord first found him by guiding the prophet Samuel to anoint him.

> "Then you spoke in a vision to your faithful one, and said: 'I have set the crown on one who is mighty, I have exalted one chosen from the people. I have found (*heyriskō*) my servant David; with my holy oil I have anointed him;'" Psalm 89:19-20

The prophet Isaiah conveys a beautiful message from the Lord to the lost sheep of Israel in Isaiah 65.

> "I was ready to be sought out by those who did not ask, to be found (*heyriskō*) by those who did not seek me. I said, 'Here I am, here I am,' to a nation that did not call on my name." Isaiah 65:1

Despite Israel's lack of active pursuit, the Lord remains available to be discovered. Like a game of hide and seek where the child barely conceals themselves behind a tree, He eagerly desires the seeker's love. This verse carries profound implications regarding God's accessibility and His deep desire to be found by His people.

The Lord has always made Himself discoverable. Jeremiah echoes the words of God as he prophesied to the people of Israel, saying:

> "When you search for me, you will find (*heyriskō*) me; if you seek me with all

your heart, I will let you find me, says the Lord, and I will restore your fortunes and gather you from all the nations and all the places where I have driven you, says the Lord, and I will bring you back to the place from which I sent you into exile." Jeremiah 29:13

This verse showcases the Lord's faithfulness in responding to sincere seekers, just as Jesus reminded his disciples in Matthew 7:7.

In the New Testament, Luke chapter 2 details a profound moment in which Mary and Joseph "lose" and eventually "find" Jesus in the temple. When Mary and Joseph realize that Jesus is not with them on their way back from Jerusalem, they spend three days searching.

"After three days they found (*heyriskō*) him in the temple, sitting among the teachers, listening to them and asking them questions. And all who heard him were amazed at his understanding and his answers. When his parents saw him they were astonished; and his mother said to him, 'Child, why have you treated us like this? Look, your father and I have been searching for you in great anxiety.' He said to them, 'Why were you searching for me? Did you not know that I must be in my Father's house?'" Luke 2:46-49

This early story of Jesus's life as a boy is such a beautiful reversal of the Parable of the Prodigal Son. Where the son is lost wandering away from the father, Jesus is lost seeking the Father. Even at this young age, Jesus is already aware of His relationship with God, desiring every moment with Him.

At the end of Peter's second letter to the Churches in Asia Minor, he closes by recalling the promise of a new heaven and new earth, where righteousness is our home. He encourages holiness and godliness while awaiting Christ's return writing:

"Therefore, beloved, while you are waiting for these things, strive to be found (*heyriskō*) by him at peace, without spot or blemish; and regard the patience of our Lord as salvation..." 2 Peter 3:14-15

The passages, ranging from the Psalms of praise to the hope in Peter's letter, all resonate with the theme of seeking and finding in the context of a personal and transformative encounter with God. He is not only accessible but also eagerly awaits discovery.

As we earnestly seek the Lord, we will discover His faithfulness, compassion, and unfailing love. He invites us to actively seek Him sincerely and wholeheartedly, assuring that our search will never be in vain. In return, He offers reconciliation.

Reflect

... get the fatted calf and kill it, and let us eat and celebrate; for this son of mine was dead and is alive again; he was lost and is found!

Luke 15:21

on the app...

VISIT THIS SECTION'S MEDITATION VIDEO IN THE APP FOR A MOMENT OF GUIDED REFLECTION

REFLECTION FROM AN EARLY CHURCH FATHER

" Then the robe, the ring, and the shoes are brought out. The robe represents wisdom; with this robe the apostles cover the body's nakedness; each one is wrapped in it. They receive the robe to clothe the frailty of their body with the force of spiritual wisdom…

The ring is the seal of sincere faith and the stamp of truth. The shoes have reference to the preaching of the Gospel (cf.Ep 6:15). Notice that the son received the "first robe", the first wisdom - for there is another sort of wisdom that is ignorant of the mystery; he received the seal in words and in acts. And he received a guarantee that he would continue in his good intentions and along the right course, so that he would not trip up on a stone and injure himself. For, were the devil to cause him to tumble, he would leave off preaching the Gospel of the Lord. These shoes he was given are "the preparation of the Gospel" (cf.Ep 6:15) that send people out on the course directed towards heavenly goods; with such shoes we do not walk according to the flesh, but according to the spirit (cf.Rm 8:4)…

Those who have the ring have the Father, the Son, and the Holy Spirit for on them God has made His mark. God, of whom Christ is the Image has stamped this mark upon us; He has sealed us and given us the pledge of the Spirit in our hearts; that we might know that such is the seal of this ring which is given into our hand, and which is imprinted on our hearts, our actions, and our ministry. So, we have been stamped and sealed. It is as we have read: "You who believe have been signed with the Holy Spirit" (Ep 1:13).

- St. Ambrose, *Exposition on the Gospel of St. Luke*, Book VII (377 AD)

As you ponder these verses, journal your thoughts in the space provided. Reflect on the scripture passage (and subsequent supporting passages) from "Read." Is there a word that stands out? What do these verses mean to you? What is the Holy Spirit showing you in these scripture passages?

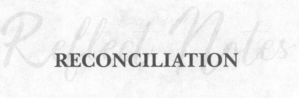

RECONCILIATION

Image: The font where Augustine was baptize
San Giovanni alle Fonti in Milan. Credit: A nt
CC BY-SA 3.0, via Wikimedia Commons

Respond

In this section, we will continue our look at Augustine of Hippo and his response to God's word. May it serve as example as you seek out how the Holy Spirit is prompting you to Respond.

IN THE FATHER'S EMBRACE

During his moment in the garden, Augustine was not alone. His friend Alypius witnessed the extraordinary emotional roller coaster from a distance. Alypius, who also sought truth, was inspired by Augustine's transformation.

In asking to see what Augustine had read, Alypius reads aloud the following line from Romans 14:1 "Welcome those who are weak in faith…"

"He referred this text to himself and interpreted it to me. Confirmed by this admonition he associated himself with my decision and purpose without any upheaval or delay…"[2]

Like eager children with exciting news, Augustine and Alypius run inside to tell Monica, who is overjoyed.

"When we related to her how it happened she was filled with triumphant delight and blessed you, you have power to do more than we ask or understand."[3]

Augustine instantly drops the last of his burdens as he resolves to leave his position as a teacher of rhetoric.

"I believed it to be pleasing in your sight that I should withdraw the service of my tongue from the market of speechifying, so that young boys…

should no longer buy from my mouth the weapons of their frenzy."[4]

Augustine rests in the embrace of the Father, free from shackles stranded on the road. He assumes a new identity, not as an intellectual who has pridefully found "the truth," but as a lost son who humbly found his home by submitting to the Father's good will.

"How sweet did it suddenly seem to me to shrug off those sweet frivolities, and how glad I now was to get rid of them— I who has been loath to let them go! For it was you who cast them out from me, you, our real and all-surpassing sweetness. You cast them out and entered yourself to take their place, you who are lovelier than any pleasure, though not to flesh and blood, more lustrous than any light, yet more inward than is any secret intimacy, loftier than all honor, yet not to those who look for loftiness in themselves. My mind was free at last from the gnawing need to seek advancement and riches, to welter in filth and scratch my itching lust. Childlike, I chattered away to you, my glory, my wealth, my salvation, and my Lord and God."[5]

To be received into the Church, Augustine, and Alypius would make their public confession and be baptized during the Easter Vigil. In a joyous addition, Augustine's son Adeodatus joins them as they spend their months praying and reading scripture with new resolve. During this time, Augustine consumes himself in the Psalms, particularly Psalm 4.

> "I read the fourth Psalm in that place of peace. *When I called on him he heard me, the God of my vindication; when I was hard beset you led me into spacious freedom. Have mercy on me, Lord, and hearken to my prayer*... I shuttered with awe, yet all the while hope and joy surged up within me at your mercy."[6]

This serenity causes Augustine to pity the Manichees. He wishes they could know the reason for the happiness on his face and ease in his voice. Yet he knows they would be unable to observe the internal thoughts and feelings that moved him.

> "For me, good things were no longer outside, no longer quested for by fleshly eyes in the world's sunlight. Those who want to find their joy in externals all too easily grow empty themselves. They pour themselves out on things which, being seen, are but transient, and lick even the images of these things with their famished imagination. If only they would weary of their starvation and ask, 'Who will show us good things?'"[7]

Augustine, who had eaten of those earthly goods, triumphed in abandoning them for a different "wheat and wine and oil."[8]

Augustine writes to him and Alypius's former roommate, Nebridius. Just like with Alypius, Augustine had led him into Manichaeism and was now writing to convince him of the truth in Christ. He hoped dearly that Nebridius would join him and Alypius by sharing to him the satisfaction to which he gladly testified. Although it wouldn't be during this time, Nebridius eventually converted and became a Christian, inspiring all his household to follow as well.

At the Easter Vigil on April 24th, 387 AD, Augustine, Alypius, and Augustine's son Adeodatus were baptized in Milan by Bishop Ambrose. Ambrose's book *On the Mysteries*, transports the reader to the 4th century Easter Vigil. The bishop eloquently reflects on the benefits received by those baptized, the rites themselves, and the meaning of the Sacrament.

Ambrose begins by recounting how those entering the Church are encouraged to be open to the savior of internal life, with the priest stating: "*Ephphatha*, which is, Be opened, Mark 7:34."

The catechumens then turn themselves to the East.

> "After this the Holy of holies was opened to you, you entered the sanctuary of regeneration; recall what you were asked, and remember what you answered. You renounced the devil and his works, the world with its luxury and pleasures. That utterance of yours is preserved not in the tombs of the dead, but in the book of the living."[9]

The believers are then submerged in water.

> "You went down, then (into the water), remember what you replied to the questions, that you believe in the Father, that you believe in the Son, that you believe in the Holy Spirit. The statement there is not: I believe in a greater and in a less and in a lowest person, but you are bound by the same guarantee of your own voice, to believe in the Son in like manner as you believe in the Father; and to believe in the Holy Spirit in like manner as you believe in the Son, with this one exception, that

you confess that you must believe in the cross of the Lord Jesus alone."[10]

After this, the baptized walk up to the priest to be anointed with oil.

"Consider now why this is done, for the eyes of a wise man are in his head; Ecclesiastes 2:14 therefore the ointment flows down to the beard, that is to say, to the beauty of youth; and therefore, Aaron's beard, that we, too, may become a chosen race, priestly and precious, for we are all anointed with spiritual grace for a share in the kingdom of God and in the priesthood."[11]

After the anointing with oil, their feet are washed by the priests.

"Observe at the same time that the mystery consists in the very office of humility, for Christ says: If I, your Lord and Master, have washed your feet; how much more ought you to wash one another's feet. For, since the Author of Salvation Himself redeemed us through His obedience, how much more ought we His servants to offer the service of our humility and obedience."[12]

After this, the faithful are given white robes as a sign of innocence.

"But Christ, beholding His Church, for whom He Himself, as you find in the book of the prophet Zechariah, had put on filthy garments, now clothed in white raiment, seeing, that is, a soul pure and washed in the laver of regeneration, says: *Behold, you are fair, My love, behold you are fair, your eyes are like a dove's*, Song of Songs 4:1 in the likeness of which the Holy Spirit descended from heaven."[13]

It's then they receive the seal of the Holy Spirit.

... "the spirit of wisdom and understanding, the spirit of counsel and strength, the spirit of knowledge and godliness, and the spirit of holy fear, Isaiah 11:2 and preserved what you received. God the Father sealed you, Christ the Lord strengthened you, and gave the earnest of the Spirit in your heart, 2 Corinthians 5:5 as you have learned in the lesson from the Apostle."[14]

The new members of the Church then receive Christ in the Eucharist.

"Christ, then, feeds His Church with these sacraments, by means of which the substance of the soul is strengthened... So, then, having obtained everything, let us know that we are born again, but let us not say, How are we born again? Have we entered a second time into our mother's womb and been born again? ... If, then, the Holy Spirit coming down upon the Virgin wrought the conception, and effected the work of generation, surely we must not doubt but that, coming down upon the Font, or upon those who receive Baptism, He effects the reality of the new birth."[15]

Augustine, fully reconciled with the Father, weeps at the sounds of hymns and canticles, intensely moved by the lovely harmonies. These hymns became Augustine's welcome feast, fatten calf, ring, and robe.

"Those voices flooded my ears, and the truth was distilled into my heart until it overflowed in loving devotion; my tears ran down, and I was the better for them."[16]

QUESTIONS

1. List some things Augustine was inspired to do once reconciled with the Father?

2. What elements of the Easter Vigil stood out to you the most?

3. How did Augustine feel after his baptism?

4. How similar is Augustine's conversion to conversion stories today? Any differences?

5. Can you relate your own spiritual journey to Augustine's story?

6. What ways can you help bring others into the Father's embrace?

"When you search for me, you will find me; if you seek me with all your heart, I will let you find me, says the Lord, and I will restore your fortunes and gather you from all the nations and all the places where I have driven you, says the Lord, and I will bring you back to the place from which I sent you into exile."

JEREMIAH 29:13 (NSRV

Image: The view of Jerusalem from the Kidron Valley, Israel

Rest

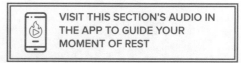

VISIT THIS SECTION'S AUDIO IN THE APP TO GUIDE YOUR MOMENT OF REST

As you finish this part of the study, visit the mobile app for this section's Rest meditation song. Additionally, below for you to meditate on is an excerpt from Augustine's *Confessions* about the nature of God as we seek to understand the forgiveness He offers.

WHAT ARE YOU, THEN, MY GOD?

What are you, then, my God? What are you, I ask, but the Lord God? For who else is lord except the Lord, or who is god if not our God?

You are most high, excellent, most powerful, omnipotent, supremely merciful and supremely just, most hidden yet intimately present, infinitely beautiful and infinitely strong, steadfast yet elusive, unchanging yourself though you control the change in all things, never new, never old, renewing all things yet wearing down the proud though they know it not; ever active, ever at rest, gathering while knowing no need, supporting and filling and guarding, creating and nurturing and perfecting, seeking although you lack nothing.

You love without frenzy, you are jealous yet secure, you regret without sadness, you grow angry yet remain tranquil, you alter your works but never your plan: you take back what you find although you never lost it; you are never in need yet you rejoice in your gains, never avaricious yet you demand profits.

You allow us to pay you more than you demand, and so you become our debtor. Yet which of us possesses anything that does not already belong to you?

You owe us nothing, yet you pay your debts; you write off our debts to you, yet you lose nothing thereby.

**- St. Augustine of Hippo,
The Confessions, Book I,
Section 4**

PART 6 - REJOICING

Image: Sunset on the coastline of Apollonia Beach, Israel

PART 6

Rejoicing

> **66**
>
> *But we had to celebrate and rejoice, because this brother of yours was dead and has come to life; he was lost and has been found.*
>
> **LUKE 15:32 (NRSV)**

Image: *Triumph of the Name of Jesus* by Giovanni Battista Gaulli in Chiesa del Gesù, Rome, Italy

Read

DEEP DIVE INTO SCRIPTURE

Read Luke 15:25-32 "… But we had to celebrate and rejoice, because this brother of yours was dead and has come to life; he was lost and has been found." To dig further into verses 25-32, continue to look at supporting verses from both the Old and New Testaments that include "rejoice" (*chairō*). Using your preferred translation and make note of any different English words found.

Word / Phrase	Verse	Write Out His Word
be glad, joy, exult, rejoice (English) chairō (Greek)	Psalm 96: 11-13	
	Zechariah 9:9	
	John 8:56	
	John 14:28	
	Romans 12:15-16	

AN EASTER PEOPLE

In the Parable of the Prodigal Son, Jesus goes beyond making the story just about returning the lost to the Father. He extends the narrative to teach the Pharisees, who had questioned his association with tax collectors and sinners, about their role in the story.

Jesus reveals that not only is he dining with the outcasts to reconcile them to the Father, but the Pharisees, like the elder son, should find joy in this divine mission.

Joining the rhythmic drumbeat of "lost" (*apollymi*) and "found" (*heyriskō*) is the word "rejoice." In Greek, *chairō* (pronounced khah'-ee-ro) is used for rejoice. It conveys the idea of greeting someone with great joy and celebration.[1]

chairō - to be glad, rejoice, to be merry, joyful greeting

A well-known example of this greeting can be found in the story of the Annunciation in Luke 1:28. The angel Gabriel announces "Hail Mary" with *chairō*:

> "Greetings (*chairō*), favored one! The Lord is with you." Luke 1:28

How fearful Mary must have been at the sight of the angel, while the angel expresses great excitement with *chairō* at seeing her!

Many verses in scripture speak of heaven and creation rejoicing and how we are to join in that triumphant praise. In Psalm 96, the psalmist King David calls for a universal celebration and rejoicing in the presence of the Lord.

> "Let the heavens be glad, and let the earth rejoice; let the sea roar, and all that fills it; let the field exult (*chairō*),

and everything in it. Then shall all the trees of the forest sing for joy before the Lord; for he is coming, for he is coming to judge the earth." Psalm 96:11-13

The passage depicts a vibrant scene where all creation is welcome to participate in joyful adoration. Even the fields join in the song of joy before the Lord. This exuberant imagery emphasizes the all-encompassing nature of God's reign and the overflowing happiness that should fill our hearts as we recognize His sovereignty.

Turning to the book of Zechariah, chapter 9 contains a prophetic message about the arrival of the Messiah. In this passage, the prophet foretells the triumphant and victorious entry of the king to come.

> "Rejoice (*chairō*) greatly, O daughter Zion! Shout aloud, O daughter Jerusalem! Lo, your king comes to you; triumphant and victorious is he, humble and riding on a donkey, on a colt, the foal of a donkey." Zechariah 9:9

The fact that Jesus came, as the Son of God, to be the Son of Man to restore that road to the Father is a cause for tremendous celebration. Jesus himself states this beautifully by saying:

> "Your ancestor Abraham rejoiced that he would see my day; he saw it and was glad (*chairō*)." John 8:56

It's a beautiful thought to think of Abraham and the prophets rejoicing at the news of Jesus's birth. In their earthly lives, they had only glimpsed God's plan without fully understanding it. Now, because of Christ, they will receive their heavenly place.

As followers of Christ, we are to celebrate

and rejoice in God's redemption of others. In Romans 12, the apostle Paul instructs us,

> "Rejoice (*chairō*) with those who rejoice (*chairō*), weep with those who weep. Live in harmony with one another; do not be haughty, but associate with the lowly; do not claim to be wiser than you are." Romans 12:15

Pope John Paul II likely quoted St. Augustine of Hippo when he said, "We are an Easter People, and Alleluia is our song!"[2] Augustine explains in his commentary on Psalm 148 that we should praise the Lord in all we do. Whether fasting or praying, we should always remember the Lord's resurrection and ours to come. Augustine writes, 'Halleluia. Praise the Lord,' you say to your neighbor, he to you: when all are exhorting each other, all are doing what they exhort others to do. But praise with your whole selves: that is, let not your tongue and voice alone praise God, but your conscience also, your life, your deeds."[3]

Despite being called to celebrate, we often burden ourselves unnecessarily by focusing on unsatisfied desires. If we have reconciled with the Father, we possess all we need. There is no need to adopt the elder son's attitude in the parable. Instead, we rejoice, celebrate, and believe the Father when he assures us, "All I have is yours."

It's easy to be consumed by only what we can see. Jesus understood this as he told his disciples:

> "You heard me say to you, 'I am going away, and I am coming to you.' If you loved me, you would rejoice (*chairō*) that I am going to the Father, because the Father is greater than I." John 14:28

Through Jesus' sacrificial love, we can find contentment in his reunion with the Father and eagerly anticipate our eternal home with joy.

The apostle John's Book of Revelation is filled with cause for celebration as he predicts the return of Christ.

> "Let us rejoice (*chairō*) and exult and give him the glory, for the marriage of the Lamb has come, and his bride has made herself ready;" Revelation 19:7

All these verses from the Old and New Testaments serve as reminders of the invitation to celebrate God's redemptive work. They inspire us to never forget with joyful anticipation that Christ will come again.

Furthermore, we should partake in the celebration of those who are on their way home to reunion with the Father. It is a time for rejoicing, as depicted in the parable with the feast and fattened calf. Let your heart fill with gladness as you witness God's redemptive work in others' lives.

Reflect

on the app . . .

VISIT THIS SECTION'S MEDITATION VIDEO IN THE APP FOR A MOMENT OF GUIDED REFLECTION

But we had to celebrate and rejoice, because this brother of yours was dead and has come to life; he was lost and has been found.
Luke 15:32

REFLECTION FROM AN EARLY CHURCH FATHER

" The passage that follows disposes us to look with a kindly eye on those who do penance for their sins and receive pardon. If we were ungracious towards those who are pardoned, we would be in grave danger of not obtaining pardon from the Lord for ourselves. Who are you to dare question the Lord regarding His right to forgive whom He wishes? Do not you yourselves forgive those whom you wish to forgive? He likes to be asked. He likes to be asked most insistently. If everyone were to be innocent, what chance would God have to show mercy? Who are you to envy God His rights?

That is why the father finds fault with the elder brother when he comes back from his work in the farm. This man was, you see, occupied in working on the land; and ignorant of that which pertains to the Spirit of God. He complained that no one ever killed so much as a kid for him; for it is not through envy, but to take away the sins of the world, that the Lamb is slain. The envious fellow demands a kid; the innocent person desires only that the Lamb be immolated for him. We know that this brother was the elder of the two. Envy makes people grow old more quickly. If he insists on staying outside, it is because his own malice and spite exclude him from the family. He cannot bear the singing and the dancing this was not the sort of theatrical music that excites the passions, nor was it the sound of flute playing. No, it was the sweet harmony of people who sing with resounding joy at the sight of a sinner who has been saved…

For within the Church there is a symphony. People of every age and versed in every sort of virtue sing together in perfect harmony, like so many strings of the harp. Like choirs, they sing the psalms - one choir alternating with the other - and utter the great Amen… This is, at any rate, my way of explaining the present parable.

- St. Ambrose, *Exposition on the Gospel of St. Luke*, Book VII (377 AD)

As you ponder these verses, journal your thoughts in the space provided. Reflect on the scripture passage (and subsequent supporting passages) from "Read." Is there a word that stands out? What do these verses mean to you? What is the Holy Spirit showing you in these scripture passages?

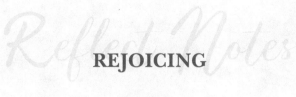

REJOICING

Image: Ancient Ostia, Italy, where Monica and Augustine shared their final moments

Respond

In this section, we will continue our look at Augustine of Hippo and his response to God's word. May it serve as example as you seek out how the Holy Spirit is prompting you to Respond.

A HEART AT REST

Reconciled with the Father, Augustine can't help but rejoice with hymns, crying tears of joy and regret. He recalls a year prior when Ambrose, his mother and the rest of the church kept vigil in response to a threat from the emperor's mother, Justina, an Arian Christian.

As all in the church prepared to die with their bishop, the parishioners and Monica sang hymns of praise to God. Augustine laments that he and his companions were not with them. Not fully yet committed to the Lord, he had missed this event.

"Yet at that time, though the fragrance of your ointments blew so freely abroad, we did not run after you; and that was why I wept the more abundantly later on when your hymns were sung…"[4]

Despite the regret, Augustine is in a place of rest. His soul is satisfied with tremendous peace.

"For me, good things were no longer outside, no longer quested for by fleshly eyes in this world's sunlight. Those who want to find their joy in externals all too easily grow empty themselves… Let us answer them, and let them hear the truth: The light of your countenance has set its seal upon us, O Lord. We are not ourselves that Light which illuminates every human being, but by you we are illumined, so that we who were once darkness may become light in you."[5]

In his *Confessions*, Augustine recalls the story of another prominent Roman teacher of rhetoric, Victorinus, who had abandoned his career so that he may be a Christian. This story was instrumental to Augustine's conversion. He celebrates him joyfully by recounting the transformation's impact on him.

Victorinus, much like Augustine, had made an intellectual conversion to follow Christ, "[he] was in the habit of reading holy scriptures and intensively studying all the Christian writing."[6] Victorinus would often call himself a Christian but had never stepped foot in a church.

Victorinus was initially too concerned about how it would appear to his friends. Ashamed by this and eventually through a change of heart, the famous rhetorician agrees to attend Christ's Church. From that moment, Victorinus changes and fully steeps into the faith.

In Rome, at that time, a confession of faith was to be made publicly in the presence of the baptized community. Knowing that this man was a very prominent figure in the Roman Senate, the priests gave him the option of a private confession. Though it may cost him his lofty profession as Emperor Julian was purging Christian teachers from schools during this time, Victorinus refuses.

> "What he taught in rhetoric was not salvation, he said, yet he had professed that publicly enough."[7]

As he climbed the platform to publicly repeat The Creed,

> "all shouted his name to one another in clamorous outburst of thanksgiving… he proclaimed the true faith, and all the people longed to clasp him tenderly to their hearts. And so they did, by loving him and rejoicing with him, for those affections were like clasping hands."[8]

All these celebrated men were examples of God's holiness to Augustine, yet, it's his mother Monica that has the most significant influence on his joy. Augustine dedicates the majority of the ninth book in *The Confessions* to her death.

Shortly after Augustine's conversion, at age thirty-three, his mother Monica, his son Adeodatus and his brothers in Christ desire to live as a quiet commune. Monica becomes a mother to them all and an example of spiritual joy and peacemaking.

Agreeing to locate this commune in Thagaste, they travel to the beautiful seaside of Ostia, Italy in order to sail to Northern Africa. Augustine recalls a moment in Ostia when he and his mother reflected on "what the eternal life of the saints would be like."[9]

> "As we talked and panted for it, we just touched the edge of it by the utmost leap of our hearts; then, sighing and unsatisfied, we left the first-fruits of our spirits captive there, and returned to the noise of articulate speech, where a word has beginning and end."[10]

In this mystic experience of glimpsing heaven, Monica and Augustine share a special moment. They conclude that the joy of the Lord alone is the only thing worth of existence. They had glimpsed and felt it in their meditative silence, leaving them wanting more. Augustine poetically writes:

> "If this could last, and all other visions, so far inferior be taken away and this sight alone ravish him who saw it, and engulf him and hide him away, kept for inward joys, so that this moment of knowledge—this passing moment that left us aching for more—should there be life eternal, would not '*Enter into the joy of your Lord*' be this, and this alone?"[11]

Monica confides in her son that her desires for anything in this world have gone cold. "I find pleasure no longer in anything this life holds… One thing only there was for which I desired to linger awhile in this life: to see you a Catholic Christian before I died. And this my God has granted me more lavishly than I could have hoped, letting me see you even spurning earthly happiness to be his servant. What now keeps me here?"[12]

Just three days after this admission, she succumbs to an illness and passes. All her earthly and spiritual sons are overcome with sadness. However, it is only a short time until their sorrow quickly turns to praise.

> "All of us in the house joined in: I will sing to you of your mercy and justice, O Lord."[13]

Augustine wrestles with this bittersweet sadness. He recovers from despair, remembering her love of the Lord, her attitude toward others, and her endless sacrificial prayers for him.

> "I found comfort in weeping before you [Lord] about her and for her, about myself and for myself."[14]

Monica was more than just his mother. She was an advocate for his salvation.

> "She brought me forth from her flesh to birth in this temporal light, and from her heart to birth in light eternal."[15]

Augustine also loses his son Adeodatus just a few years later. Yet, Augustine is at peace, recalling,

> "I have no fear about anything in his boyhood or adolescence; indeed I fear nothing whatever for that man... Nothing did I contribute to that boy's making except my fault. It was you [Lord], and you alone, who had inspired us to instruct him in your truth as he grew up, and so it is your own gifts that I acknowledge to you."[16]

Augustine follows through with establishing a semi-monastic life with his brethren in Thagaste. Yet, upon a visit to Hippo at the age of thirty-seven, he is persuaded to become a priest and, shortly after that, Bishop of Hippo. In Hippo, far from his friends but close to his memories, he pens *The Confessions*. Although a confession can imply an admission of sin, it can also mean a confession of praise— *Confitebor tibi Domine,* meaning "I will praise you, Lord"—which seems more fitting.

Throughout the rest of his life, Augustine serves as a prolific writer and influence in the establishment of Church Doctrine. Despite his tremendous impact on the faith, Augustine's most notable accomplishment is in being a recipient of God's mercy and grace. That is the point of his *Confessions* and later life of service, a sacrifice so others will praise the Father.

> "Let me offer you a sacrifice of praise, for you have snapped my bonds. How you broke them I will relate, so that all your worshipers who hear my tale may exclaim, 'Blessed be the Lord, blessed in heaven and on earth, for great and wonderful is his name.'"[17]

In the year of Augustine's death, the Vandals, an Arian Christian tribe, invaded Northern Africa. In their conquest, they laid siege to Hippo. As battles raged around him, Augustine requests the Psalms of David be mounted on the walls so he can pray and weep in praise.

On August 28th, 430 AD, Augustine was welcomed home by the Father. After Augustine passed, the Vandals breached the city of Hippo. In nothing short of a miracle, everything was destroyed except Augustine's library.

Now from his eternal rest, Augustine encourages us to seek after the Father, to run home and rest in His presence.

> "Some of our works are indeed good, thanks to your Gift, but they will not last forever, and when they are done, we hope that we shall rest in your immense holiness. But you, the supreme Good, need no other good and are eternally at rest, because you yourself are your rest. What human can empower another human to understand these things? What angel can grant understanding to another angel? What angel to a human? Let us rather ask of you, seek in you, knock at your door. Only so will we receive, only so find, and only so will the door be opened to us. Amen."[18]

QUESTIONS

1. What are some words from Augustine that indicate his heart is at rest?

2. Why does Monica's death result in praise from Augustine?

3. How do you think Augustine would want to be remembered?

4. Have you witnessed times when repentant sinners are not celebrated? Why do you think?

5. What allows us to view death as a reason to rejoice?

6. What ways can you find rest in the Father while still here on earth?

"Let the heavens be glad, and let the earth rejoice; let the sea roar, and all that fills it; let the field exult, and everything in it."

PSALM 96:11 (NSRV)

Image: The ruins of ancient Hippo and St. Augustine Basilica, Annaba, Algeria. Credit: Kris Hellstrom, Director ASA Cultural Tours

Rest

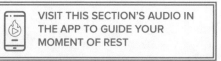
VISIT THIS SECTION'S AUDIO IN THE APP TO GUIDE YOUR MOMENT OF REST

As you finish this study, visit the mobile app for this section's Rest meditation song. Additionally, below for you to meditate on is an excerpt from Augustine's *Confessions* about true joy in the Father.

JOYFUL FATHER

O God, who are so good, what is it in the human heart that makes us rejoice more intensely over the salvation of a soul which is despaired of but then freed from grave danger, than we would if there had always been good prospects for it and its peril slighter?

You too, merciful Father, yes, even you are more joyful over one repentant sinner than over ninety-nine righteous people who need no repentance.

And we likewise listen with over-flowing gladness when we hear how the shepherd carries back on exultant shoulders the sheep that had strayed, and how the coin is returned to your treasury as neighbors share the glee of the woman who found it, while the joy of your eucharistic assembly wrings tears from us when the story is read in your house of a younger son who was dead, but has come back to life, was lost but is found.

You express your own joy through ours, and through the joy of your angels who are made holy by their holy charity; for you yourself are ever the same, and all transient things, things which cannot abide constantly in their mode of being, are known to your unchanging intelligence.

- St. Augustine of Hippo,
***The Confessions*, Book VIII, Section 6**

Endnotes

INTRODUCTION

1. Augustine. "Book 8 – Conversion." *The Confessions*. Translated by Maria Boulding, 2nd ed., New City Press, 2022, pp. 206.

2. Augustine. "Book 8 – Conversion." *The Confessions*. Translated by Maria Boulding, 2nd ed., New City Press, 2022, pp. 207.

3. Augustine. "Introduction." *The Confessions*. Translated by Maria Boulding, 2nd ed., New City Press, 2022, pp. 9.

4. Wills, Garry. *Saint Augustine*. Penguin Books, 2005.

PART 1: LOST SPACES

1. Definition of "apollymi," Blue Letter Bible, accessed on August 13, 2023, available online via blueletterbible.org/lexicon/g622/lxx/lxx/0-1/

2. Augustine. "Book 1 – Infancy and Boyhood." *The Confessions*. Translated by Maria Boulding, 2nd ed., New City Press, 2022, pp. 1.

3. Augustine. "Book 1 – Infancy and Boyhood." *The Confessions*. Translated by Maria Boulding, 2nd ed., New City Press, 2022, pp. 48.

4. Augustine. "Book 1 – Infancy and Boyhood." *The Confessions*. Translated by Maria Boulding, 2nd ed., New City Press, 2022, pp. 50.

5. Augustine. "Book 1 – Infancy and Boyhood." *The Confessions*. Translated by Maria Boulding, 2nd ed., New City Press, 2022, pp. 52.

6. Augustine. *The Confessions*. Translated by Maria Boulding, 2nd ed., New City Press, 2022, pp. 53.

7. Augustine. "Book 1 – Infancy and Boyhood." *The Confessions*. Translated by Maria Boulding, 2nd ed., New City Press, 2022, pp. 59.

8. Augustine. "Book 1 – Infancy and Boyhood." *The Confessions*. Translated by Maria Boulding, 2nd ed., New City Press, 2022, pp. 57. (Book 1, section 16)

9. Augustine. "Book 3 – Student Years at Carthage." *The Confessions*. Translated by Maria Boulding, 2nd ed., New City Press, 2022, pp. 75.

10.10 Augustine. "Book 2 – Adolescence." *The Confessions*. Translated by Maria Boulding, 2nd ed., New City Press, 2022, pp. 66.

11. Augustine. "Book 2 – Adolescence." *The Confessions*. Translated by Maria Boulding, 2nd ed., New City Press, 2022, pp. 67.

12. Augustine. "Book 2 – Adolescence." *The Confessions*. Translated by Maria Boulding, 2nd ed., New City Press, 2022, pp. 70.

13. Augustine. "Book 2 – Adolescence." *The Confessions*. Translated by Maria Boulding, 2nd ed., New City Press, 2022, pp. 71.

14. Augustine. "Book 3 – Student Years at Carthage." *The Confessions*. Translated by Maria Boulding, 2nd ed., New City Press, 2022, pp. 78.

15. Augustine. "Book 3 – Student Years at Carthage." *The Confessions*. Translated by Maria Boulding, 2nd ed., New City Press, 2022, pp. 80.

PART 2: SEVERE FAMINE

1. Definition of "hystereō," Blue Letter Bible, accessed on August 13, 2023, available online via blueletterbible.org/lexicon/g5302/lxx/lxx/0-1/

2. Augustine. "Book 1 – Infancy and Boyhood." The Confessions. Translated by Maria Boulding, 2nd ed., New City Press, 2022, pp. 58.

3. Augustine. "Book 3 – Student Years at Carthage." *The Confessions*. Translated by Maria Boulding, 2nd ed., New City Press, 2022, pp. 75.

4. Augustine. "Book 3 – Student Years at Carthage." *The Confessions*. Translated by Maria Boulding, 2nd ed., New City Press, 2022, pp. 77.

5. Augustine. "Book 3 – Student Years at Carthage." *The Confessions*. Translated by Maria Boulding, 2nd ed., New City Press, 2022, pp. 81.

6. Augustine. "Book 4 – Augustine the Manichee." *The Confessions*. Translated by Maria Boulding, 2nd ed., New City Press, 2022, pp. 94.

7. Augustine. "Book 3 – Student Years at Carthage." *The Confessions*. Translated by Maria Boulding, 2nd ed., New City Press, 2022, pp. 89.

8. Augustine. "Book 4 – Augustine the Manichee." *The Confessions*. Translated by Maria Boulding, 2nd ed., New City Press,

2022, pp. 109.

9. Augustine. "Book 5 – Faustus at Carthage, Augustine to Rome and Milan." *The Confessions*. Translated by Maria Boulding, 2nd ed., New City Press, 2022, pp. 120.

10. Augustine. "Book 5 – Faustus at Carthage, Augustine to Rome and Milan." *The Confessions*. Translated by Maria Boulding, 2nd ed., New City Press, 2022, pp. 120.

11. Augustine. "Book 6 – Milan, 385: Progress, Friends, Perplexities." *The Confessions*. Translated by Maria Boulding, 2nd ed., New City Press, 2022, pp. 143.

12. Augustine. "Book 6 – Milan, 385: Progress, Friends, Perplexities." *The Confessions*. Translated by Maria Boulding, 2nd ed., New City Press, 2022, pp. 143.

13. Augustine. "Book 6 – Milan, 385: Progress, Friends, Perplexities." *The Confessions*. Translated by Maria Boulding, 2nd ed., New City Press, 2022, pp. 144.

PART 3: SHEPHER'S VOICE

1. Definition of "anistēmi," Blue Letter Bible, accessed on August 13, 2023, available online via blueletterbible.org/lexicon/g450/lxx/lxx/0-1/

2. Augustine. "Book 2 – Adolescence." *The Confessions*. Translated by Maria Boulding, 2nd ed., New City Press, 2022, pp. 66.

3. Augustine. "Book 3 – Student Years at Carthage." *The Confessions*. Translated by Maria Boulding, 2nd ed., New City Press, 2022, pp. 89.

4. Augustine. "Book 3 – Student Years at Carthage." *The Confessions*. Translated by Maria Boulding, 2nd ed., New City Press, 2022, pp. 89.

5. Augustine. "Book 3 – Student Years at Carthage." *The Confessions*. Translated by Maria Boulding, 2nd ed., New City Press, 2022, pp. 90.

6. Augustine. "Book 4 – Augustine the Manichee." *The Confessions*. Translated by Maria Boulding, 2nd ed., New City Press, 2022, pp. 96.

7. Augustine. "Book 4 – Augustine the Manichee." *The Confessions*. Translated by Maria Boulding, 2nd ed., New City Press, 2022, pp. 97.

8. Augustine. "Book 4 – Augustine the Manichee." *The Confessions*. Translated by

Maria Boulding, 2nd ed., New City Press, 2022, pp. 97.

9. Augustine. "Book 5 – Faustus at Carthage, Augustine to Rome and Milan." *The Confessions*. Translated by Maria Boulding, 2nd ed., New City Press, 2022, pp. 123.

10. Augustine. "Book 5 – Faustus at Carthage, Augustine to Rome and Milan." *The Confessions*. Translated by Maria Boulding, 2nd ed., New City Press, 2022, pp. 124.

11. Augustine. "Book 5 – Faustus at Carthage, Augustine to Rome and Milan." *The Confessions*. Translated by Maria Boulding, 2nd ed., New City Press, 2022, pp. 127.

12. Augustine. "Book 5 – Faustus at Carthage, Augustine to Rome and Milan." *The Confessions*. Translated by Maria Boulding, 2nd ed., New City Press, 2022, pp. 131.

13. Augustine. "Book 5 – Faustus at Carthage, Augustine to Rome and Milan." *The Confessions*. Translated by Maria Boulding, 2nd ed., New City Press, 2022, pp. 131.

14. Augustine. "Book 5 – Faustus at Carthage, Augustine to Rome and Milan." *The Confessions*. Translated by Maria Boulding, 2nd ed., New City Press, 2022, pp. 131.

15. Augustine. "Book 5 – Faustus at Carthage, Augustine to Rome and Milan." *The Confessions*. Translated by Maria Boulding, 2nd ed., New City Press, 2022, pp. 132.

16. Augustine. "Book 5 – Faustus at Carthage, Augustine to Rome and Milan." *The Confessions*. Translated by Maria Boulding, 2nd ed., New City Press, 2022, pp. 133.

17. Augustine. "Book 6 – Milan, 385: Progress, Friends, Perplexities." *The Confessions*. Translated by Maria Boulding, 2nd ed., New City Press, 2022, pp. 135.

PART 4: COMING HOME

1. Definition of "splagchnizomai," Blue Letter Bible, accessed on August 13, 2023, available online via blueletterbible.org/lexicon/g4697/lxx/lxx/0-1/

2. Definition of "oiktirmos," Blue Letter Bible, accessed on August 13, 2023, available online via blueletterbible.org/lexicon/g3628/lxx/lxx/0-1/

3. Augustine. "Book 6 – Milan, 385: Progress, Friends, Perplexities." *The Confessions*. Translated by Maria Boulding, 2nd ed., New City Press, 2022, pp. 137.

Endnotes cont.

4. Augustine. "Book 6 – Milan, 385: Progress, Friends, Perplexities." *The Confessions.* Translated by Maria Boulding, 2nd ed., New City Press, 2022, pp. 139.

5. Augustine. "Book 6 – Milan, 385: Progress, Friends, Perplexities." *The Confessions.* Translated by Maria Boulding, 2nd ed., New City Press, 2022, pp. 140.

6. Augustine. "Book 6 – Milan, 385: Progress, Friends, Perplexities." *The Confessions.* Translated by Maria Boulding, 2nd ed., New City Press, 2022, pp. 142.

7. Augustine. "Book 6 – Milan, 385: Progress, Friends, Perplexities." *The Confessions.* Translated by Maria Boulding, 2nd ed., New City Press, 2022, pp. 150-151.

8. Augustine. "Book 6 – Milan, 385: Progress, Friends, Perplexities." *The Confessions.* Translated by Maria Boulding, 2nd ed., New City Press, 2022, pp. 152.

9. Augustine. "Book 6 – Milan, 385: Progress, Friends, Perplexities." *The Confessions.* Translated by Maria Boulding, 2nd ed., New City Press, 2022, pp. 156.

10. Augustine. "Book 7 – Neo-Platonism Frees Augustine's Mind." *The Confessions.* Translated by Maria Boulding, 2nd ed., New City Press, 2022, pp. 176.

11. Augustine. "Book 7 – Neo-Platonism Frees Augustine's Mind." *The Confessions.* Translated by Maria Boulding, 2nd ed., New City Press, 2022, pp. 178.

12. Augustine. "Book 7 – Neo-Platonism Frees Augustine's Mind." *The Confessions.* Translated by Maria Boulding, 2nd ed., New City Press, 2022, pp. 182.

13. Augustine. "Book 8 – Conversion." *The Confessions.* Translated by Maria Boulding, 2nd ed., New City Press, 2022, pp. 185.

14. Augustine. "Book 8 – Conversion." *The Confessions.* Translated by Maria Boulding, 2nd ed., New City Press, 2022, pp. 193.

15. Augustine. "Book 8 – Conversion." *The Confessions.* Translated by Maria Boulding, 2nd ed., New City Press, 2022, pp. 196.

16. Augustine. "Book 8 – Conversion." *The Confessions.* Translated by Maria Boulding, 2nd ed., New City Press, 2022, pp. 198.

17. Augustine. "Book 8 – Conversion." *The Confessions.* Translated by Maria Boulding, 2nd ed., New City Press, 2022, pp. 200.

18. Augustine. "Book 8 – Conversion." *The Confessions.* Translated by Maria Boulding, 2nd ed., New City Press, 2022, pp. 206.

19. Augustine. "Book 8 – Conversion." *The Confessions.* Translated by Maria Boulding, 2nd ed., New City Press, 2022, pp. 207.

PART 5: RECONCILIATION

1. Definition of "heyriskō," Blue Letter Bible, accessed on August 13, 2023, available online via blueletterbible.org/lexicon/g2147/lxx/lxx/0-1/

2. Augustine. "Book 8 – Conversion." *The Confessions.* Translated by Maria Boulding, 2nd ed., New City Press, 2022, pp. 207.

3. Augustine. "Book 8 – Conversion." *The Confessions.* Translated by Maria Boulding, 2nd ed., New City Press, 2022, pp. 207.

4. Augustine. "Book 9 – Death and Rebirth." *The Confessions.* Translated by Maria Boulding, 2nd ed., New City Press, 2022, pp. 210.

5. Augustine. "Book 9 – Death and Rebirth." *The Confessions.* Translated by Maria Boulding, 2nd ed., New City Press, 2022, pp. 210.

6. Augustine. "Book 9 – Death and Rebirth." *The Confessions.* Translated by Maria Boulding, 2nd ed., New City Press, 2022, pp. 209.

7. Augustine. "Book 9 – Death and Rebirth." *The Confessions.* Translated by Maria Boulding, 2nd ed., New City Press, 2022, pp. 215.

8. Augustine. "Book 9 – Death and Rebirth." *The Confessions.* Translated by Maria Boulding, 2nd ed., New City Press, 2022, pp. 216.

9. Augustine. "Book 9 – Death and Rebirth." *The Confessions.* Translated by Maria Boulding, 2nd ed., New City Press, 2022, pp. 217.

10. Ambrose. "On the Mysteries." *The Church Fathers–Nicene and Post-Nicene Fathers,* Second Series, Vol. 10. Edited by Philip Schaff and Henry Wace, Christian Literature Publishing Co., 1896, pp. 317.

11. Ambrose. "On the Mysteries." *The Church Fathers–Nicene and Post-Nicene Fathers,* Second Series, Vol. 10. Edited by Philip Schaff and Henry Wace, Christian Literature Publishing Co., 1896, pp. 321.

12.Ambrose. "On the Mysteries." *The Church Fathers–Nicene and Post-Nicene Fathers*, Second Series, Vol. 10. Edited by Philip Schaff and Henry Wace, Christian Literature Publishing Co., 1896, pp. 321.

13.Ambrose. "On the Mysteries." *The Church Fathers–Nicene and Post-Nicene Fathers*, Second Series, Vol. 10. Edited by Philip Schaff and Henry Wace, Christian Literature Publishing Co., 1896, pp. 321.

14.Ambrose. "On the Mysteries." *The Church Fathers–Nicene and Post-Nicene Fathers*, Second Series, Vol. 10. Edited by Philip Schaff and Henry Wace, Christian Literature Publishing Co., 1896, pp. 322.

15.Ambrose. "On the Mysteries." *The Church Fathers–Nicene and Post-Nicene Fathers*, Second Series, Vol. 10. Edited by Philip Schaff and Henry Wace, Christian Literature Publishing Co., 1896, pp. 322.

16.Ambrose. "On the Mysteries." *The Church Fathers–Nicene and Post-Nicene Fathers*, Second Series, Vol. 10. Edited by Philip Schaff and Henry Wace, Christian Literature Publishing Co., 1896, pp. 325.

17.Augustine. "Book 9 – Death and Rebirth." *The Confessions*. Translated by Maria Boulding, 2nd ed., New City Press, 2022, pp. 220.

18.Augustine. "Book 9 – Death and Rebirth." *The Confessions*. Translated by Maria Boulding, 2nd ed., New City Press, 2022, pp. 220.

SECTION 6: REJOICING

1. Definition of "chairō," Blue Letter Bible, accessed on August 13, 2023, available online via blu;letterbible.org/lexicon/g5463/lxx/lxx/0-1/

2. John Paul II. "Angelus" The Holy See, 29 Nov. 1986, www.vatican.va/content/john-paul-ii/en/angelus/1986/documents/hf_jp-ii_ang_19861130.html.

3. Augustine. "Sermon 148." *The Church Fathers–Nicene and Post-Nicene Fathers*, First Series, Vol. 8. Edited by Philip Schaff, Christian Literature Publishing Co., 1888

4. Augustine. "Book 9 – Death and Rebirth." *The Confessions*. Translated by Maria Boulding, 2nd ed., New City Press, 2022, pp. 221.

5. Augustine. "Book 9 – Death and Rebirth." *The Confessions*. Translated by Maria Boulding, 2nd ed., New City Press, 2022, pp.

216.

6. Augustine. "Book 9 – Death and Rebirth." *The Confessions*. Translated by Maria Boulding, 2nd ed., New City Press, 2022, pp. 187.

7. Augustine. "Book 9 – Death and Rebirth." *The Confessions*. Translated by Maria Boulding, 2nd ed., New City Press, 2022, pp. 189.

8. Augustine. "Book 9 – Death and Rebirth." *The Confessions*. Translated by Maria Boulding, 2nd ed., New City Press, 2022, pp. 189.

9. Augustine. "Book 9 – Death and Rebirth." *The Confessions*. Translated by Maria Boulding, 2nd ed., New City Press, 2022, pp. 227.

10.Augustine. "Book 9 – Death and Rebirth." *The Confessions*. Translated by Maria Boulding, 2nd ed., New City Press, 2022, pp. 227-228.

11.Augustine. "Book 9 – Death and Rebirth." *The Confessions*. Translated by Maria Boulding, 2nd ed., New City Press, 2022, pp. 228.

12.Augustine. "Book 9 – Death and Rebirth." *The Confessions*. Translated by Maria Boulding, 2nd ed., New City Press, 2022, pp. 229.

13.Augustine. "Book 9 – Death and Rebirth." *The Confessions*. Translated by Maria Boulding, 2nd ed., New City Press, 2022, pp. 232.

14.Augustine. "Book 9 – Death and Rebirth." *The Confessions*. Translated by Maria Boulding, 2nd ed., New City Press, 2022, pp. 233.

15.Augustine. "Book 9 – Death and Rebirth." *The Confessions*. Translated by Maria Boulding, 2nd ed., New City Press, 2022, pp. 222.

16.Augustine. "Book 9 – Death and Rebirth." *The Confessions*. Translated by Maria Boulding, 2nd ed., New City Press, 2022, pp. 219.

17.Augustine. "Book 9 – Death and Rebirth." *The Confessions*. Translated by Maria Boulding, 2nd ed., New City Press, 2022, pp. 184.

18.Augustine. "Book 13 – The Days of Creation, Prophecy of the Church." *The Confessions*. Translated by Maria Boulding, 2nd ed., New City Press, 2022, pp. 379-380.

THE
HAGIOS
STUDY

View more about The Hagios Study and follow us on
social media by visiting https://hagios.study

A special thanks to all the donors whose
support made this study possible.

Made in United States
Troutdale, OR
11/29/2023

15109288R00066